ASPECTS OF WATER LAW

Aspects
of
Water Law

by

A.S. WISDOM
SOLICITOR

BARRY ROSE PUBLISHERS . CHICHESTER. SUSSEX

© Execs. A. S. Wisdom 1981

ISBN 0-85992 - 154 - 9

Published by
BARRY ROSE (PUBLISHERS) LTD
CHICHESTER, WEST SUSSEX

Printed by EntaPrint Ltd., Cranleigh, Surrey

CONTENTS

FOREWORD

This miscellany, which illustrates the principles, rules and doctrines governing various facets of the law as it affects rivers, water rights and attendant matters, had its origins in a series of articles which appeared in the *Justice of the Peace* some twenty years ago. As now reproduced, it bears the substantial changes which have taken place mainly in the statute law concerning water since then. This work was passed for press shortly before the Author's death in the latter part of 1979.

TABLE OF CASES

Howard v Ingersoll (1851) 17 Ala 780; 54
US 427, 23, 97
Howe v Stawell (1883) Alc & N 348, 20
Hudson v Tabor (1877) 42 JP 20, 8, 24, 26,
28, 71
Hull, re, and Selby Rly (1834) 8 LJ Ex 260,
78, 81
Huzzey v Field (1835) 5 Tyr 855, 33

Ilchester (Earl) v Raishley (1889) 61 LTT
477 5 TLR 739, 38 WR 104, 19, 90
Ingram v Morecraft (1863) 33 Beav. 49, 87
Ingram v Percival (1969) 1 QB 548, 14

Johnston v O'Neill [1911] AC 552, 52, 53,
54, 90
Jolliffe v Wallasey LB (1873) 38 JP 40, 87
Jones v Llanrwst UDC (1911) 75 JP 68, 11,
58
Jones v Mersey River Board [1957] 3 All ER
375, 23
Jordeson v Sutton, Southcoates & Drypool
Gas Co (1889) 63 JP 692, 50

Kearns v Cordwainers' Co (1859) 23 JP 760,
67, 85
Kirby v Gibbs (1667) 2 Keble 274, 65

Lamb v Newbiggin (1844) 1 Car & Kir 549
NP, 96, 97
Lancashire, The (1874) 2 Asp 202, 36
Lawes v Turner (1892) 8 TLR 584, 67
Layzell v Thompson (1926) 91 JP 89, 34
Lea Conservancy Board v Button (1881) 46
JP 164, 75
Legge & Sons Ltd v Wenlock Corporation
[1938] 1 All ER 37; 102 JP 93, 12
Leith-Buchanan v Hogg [1931] SC 204, 15
Le Strange v Rowe (1866) 4 F & F 1048, 18
Letton v Gooden (1866) 30 JP 677, 33, 35, 37
Llandudno UDC v Woods (1899) 63 JP 775,
19, 21
London & NW Railway v Fobbing Levels
Commission (1896) 75 LT 629, 27
Londonderry Bridge Commissioners v
M'Keever (1890) 27 LR Ir 464, 34
Lowe v Govett (1832) 1 LJKb 224, 17
Lyme Regis Corporation v Henley (1834) 1
Scott 29, 27, 71
Lyon & Fishmongers' Co (1876) 42 JP 163,
9, 10, 67, 73, 85
Lyons & Winter (1899) 25 VLR 464, 2

MacCannon v Sinclair (1859) 23 JP 757,
52, 68
McCartney v Londonderry Co [1904] AC
301, 10
M'Intyre Brothers v M'Gavin [1893] AC 268,
12
M'Nab v Robertson [1897] AC 129 HL Sc, 2,
3, 45, 47
Magor v Chadwick (1840) 11 A & E 568, 9
LJ QB 159, 29, 32
Malcolmson v O'Dea (1863) 10 HL Cas 593,
89, 92, 93
Mansford v Ross & Glendenning (1886)
NZRCA 33, 2
Marshall v Ulleswater Steam Navigation Co
Ltd (1863) 3 B & S 732; 27 JP 516, 52, 53,
54
Marshall v Ulleswater Steam Navigation Co
(1871) 36 JP 583, 9, 54, 74
Martell v Consett Iron Co [1955] 1 All ER
481, 94
Mason v Shrewsbury & Hereford Railway
(1871) LR 6 QB 586, 76
Maxwell Wilshire v Bromley RDC (1917) 82
JP 12, 2
Mayfield v Robinson (1845) 7 QB 486, 34
Mayor of Carlisle v Graham (1869) LR 4 Ex
366, 16
Mayor of Nottingham v Lambert (1738)
Willes 111, 35
Mayor of Orford v Richardson (1791) 4 TR
473, 19
Mellor v Walmesley (1905) 93 LT 574, 17,
79, 90
Menzies v Breadlane (1828) 3 Bli NS 414,
28
Menzies v Macdonald (1856) 2 Macq 463,
54
Mercer v Denne (1905) 70 JP 65, 19, 79, 90
Merricks v Cadwallader (1881) 46 JP 216
DC, 5
Mersey Docks v Gibbs (1864) 14 LT 677, 42
Mickelthwait v Newlay Bridge Co (1886) 51
JP 132, 51
Micklethwait v Vincent (1892) 67 LT 225,
15, 54, 93
Miller v Little (1878) 4 LR Ir 302, 98

TABLE OF STATUTES

TABLE OF RULES AND REGULATIONS

.

WHAT IS A RIVER?

The use and enjoyment of water, flowing in a channel gives rise to much of the operations and problems of the water industry and we ought to know something of the characteristics of a river.

To the layman, who is probably aware that a river is a flow of natural water in a channel which leads to the sea or another river, such a question as is implied in the title above seems unnecessary. But the lawyer will regard this as a problem which can only be answered in the light of the many available decisions of the courts and statutory definitions. Most legal textbooks dealing with water commence by stating that the anatomy of a river consists of its bed, the banks and the flowing water, and it may be assumed as a matter of fact that every river has a source, such as a spring, initial tributaries or a glacier (in colder countries than Britain), to bring about the flow of water, some sort of a channel with a bed and banks or shores, to contain the flow, and a termination in tidal waters or a larger river.

Definition at Common Law. At common law a river means water flowing in a channel more or less defined, although the channel may be occasionally dry: *R.* v. *Oxfordshire (Inhabitants)* (1830) 1 B. & Ad. 289. A stream which flows in a permanently defined channel, although it is fed exclusively by rainwater running off the surface of the land and ceases to flow during a considerable part of each year, is a watercourse, and a river which naturally runs dry a good part of the year does not cease to be a river merely because at times it is accustomed to become dry: *Stollmeyer* v. *Trinidad Lake Petroleum Co.* [1918] A.C. 485. All accessories to a stream, from whatever source, form part of it: *Wood* v. *Waud* (1849) 3 Exch. 748.

Nor does a river cease to be regarded as such if it emerges from, or disappears into, the ground. The moment water of a spring issues from the ground and runs into a defined channel it constitutes a watercourse: *Dudden* v. *Clutton Union* (1857) 1 H. & N. 627. Water, which after flowing in a defined channel for a certain distance, comes lower down

1

on to a chalk bed, where the water gradually filters into and is absorbed by the chalk, is none the less a watercourse: *Maxwell Wilshire* v. *Bromley R.D.C.* (1917) 82 J.P. 12. But "bourne flows" of underground water in a chalk district, which run periodically in times of flood across the surface of the ground in a channel do not constitute a watercourse: *Pearce* v. *Croydon R.D.C.* (1910) 74 J.P. 429.

Is it always necessary that river water must flow along a marked channel? The answer to that is yes, since water which squanders itself over an undefined area is not a watercourse: *Rawstron v. Taylor* (1855) 11 Ex. 369, in which it was held that the owner of land has an unqualified right to drain it for purposes of agriculture, in order to get rid of purely surface water, the supply of water being casual and its flow following no regular or definite course, and a neighbouring proprietor cannot complain that he is thereby deprived of such water which otherwise would have come to his land. Waste water which is allowed to flow from a canal is not a watercourse, since the water in the canal is not flowing water: *Staffordshire & Worcestershire Canal Co.* v. *Birmingham Canal Co.* (1866) L.R. 1 H.L. 254.

However, this answer must be qualified. Though the word "stream" in its more usual application does imply water running between defined banks, it is not confined to that meaning — its essence being that it is water in motion as distinguished from stagnant water: *M'Nab* v. *Robertson* [1897] A.C. 129 H.L. Sc. A river may, for part of its length, lose or depart from its normal defined channel without necessarily ceasing to be regarded as a river. A New Zealand case, *Mansford v. Ross & Glendenning* (1886) 5 N.Z.R.C.A. 33, decided that where a well defined natural stream emptied into a swamp and all definite channel is lost, but emerges again into a well-defined stream below, it is a question of fact whether it is the same stream. The Australian case of *Lyons* v. *Winter* (1899) 25 V.L.R. 464 held that to constitute a watercourse, such as creates riparian rights, there must be a stream of water flowing in a defined channel or between something in the nature of banks; the stream may be very small and need not always run, nor need the banks be clearly or sharply defined, but there must be a course, marked on the earth by visible signs along which the water usually flows.

Can a stream which runs underground be considered in the same light as one running on the surface? This point has been noted in a number of cases. It appears that the principles which apply to flowing water in streams or rivers on the surface apply equally to water in a defined and known underground channel, but such principles do not relate to underground water which merely percolates through the strata in no known channels (*Chasemore* v. *Richards* (1859) 23 J.P. 596), nor to underground water flowing in a defined channel, where the existence and course of the channel are not known and cannot be ascertained except by excavation: *Bradford Corpn.* v. *Ferrand* (1902) 67 J.P. 21.

It was said in the House of Lords in *M'Nab* v. *Robertson, supra* (which decided that water percolating through the ground from marshy land to a pond was not water in a stream) that "the word" 'stream' in its primary sense denotes a body of water having, as such body, a continuous flow of water in one direction. It is frequently used to signify running water at places where its flow is rapid, as distinguished from its sluggish current in other places. I see no reason to doubt that a subterranean flow of water may in some circumstances possess the very same characteristics as a body of water running on the surface. But, water, whether falling from the sky or escaping from a spring which does not flow onward with any continuity of parts, but becomes dissipated in the earthy strata, and simply percolates through or along those strata, until it issues from them at a lower level through dislocation of the strata or otherwise, cannot be described as a stream." A watercourse which sinks underground, pursues a subterranean course for a short space and then emerges again, does not cease to be a stream: *Dickinson v. Grand Junction Canal* (1852) 7 Ex. 300.

Must a watercourse be natural? Not necessarily, for a watercourse, originally artificial, may, by reason of the circumstances under which it was made and the manner in which it has been used by riparian owners, assume the attributes of a natural watercourse (*Sutcliffe* v. *Booth* (1863) 27 J.P. 613), and where a watercourse is partially artificial and partly natural, so that no one can tell where the artificial part was constructed, the watercourse must be deemed to be a natural watercourse: *Roberts* v. *Richards* (1881) 44 L.T. 271. On the other hand, an artificial stream of a temporary character, having its continuance only whilst the convenience of its owners required it, is not a natural watercourse: *Arkwright* v. *Gell* (1839) 2 H. & H. 17. When considering the statutory definitions of "river," etc., later, it will be observed that, generally speaking, they may be either natural or artificial.

Rivers, other than those which are purely tributaries, eventually join the sea, and their waters become subject to the flow of the tide. Must they then be regarded as being part of the sea and cease to be rivers? Quite clearly, no. If navigable, the tidal part of the river becomes a public navigable river, and although there are important legal distinctions between tidal and non-tidal rivers as regards fishing, navigation, ownership of the bed, etc., a river does not cease to be a watercourse below the point at which the tide ebbs and flows. A tidal river may be included in the term "watercourse" (*Somersetshire Drainage Comrs.* v. *Bridgewater Corpn.* (1900) 81 L.T. 729, H.L.), and the mouth of a river comprehends the whole space between the lowest ebb and the highest flood mark: *Horne* v. *Mackenzie* (1839) 2 Cl. & Fin. 628.

The word "watercourse" in a grant may mean either an easement or right to the running of water, or the channel through which the water runs, or the land over which the water flows. The meaning in each case must be determined by the context: *Taylor* v. *St. Helen's Corpn.* (1877) 37 L.T. 253. In *Doe d. Egremont (Earl)* v. *Williams* (1848) 12 Jur. 455, the word "watercourse" reserved in a lease was taken to be the stream and flow of the water and not the channel through which it flowed.

The cases quoted above give some indication of the attitude adopted by the courts in determining whether a flow of water in any particular circumstances constitutes a river. In *Briscoe* v. *Drought* (1860) Ir. R. 11 C.L. 264, it was stated that where the question at a trial is whether there is a watercourse or not, the judge ought, before he leaves the question for the jury, to instruct them as to what constitutes a watercourse at law.

Statutory Definitions and References. The statutes employ different terms to denote a river, such as "watercourse", "stream" or "river" and their definitions vary according to the Acts concerned.

The **Water Act, 1945,** s.59(1) (and also s.1 of sch. 3 to that Act) give a meaning to "watercourse" which closely resembles that definition assigned by other Acts referred to herein, namely " . . . includes all rivers, streams, ditches, drains, cuts, culverts, dykes, sluices, sewers (other than sewers vested in a local authority or a water authority) and passages, through which water flows".

The **Land Drainage Act, 1976,** uses the term "watercourse", which is defined by s.116(1) to include "all rivers, streams, ditches, drains, cuts, culverts, dykes, sluices, sewers (other than public sewers within the meaning of the Public Health Act 1936) and passages, through which water flows". In *Bowes* v. *Watson* (1879) 44 J.P. 364, the words "drain, stream or watercourse" which appeared in the Land Drainage Act, 1847, were held not to be restricted to open watercourses and included an underground drain. The expression "main river", defined by s.8(3) of the 1976 Act, refers to those watercourses under the jurisdiction of a water authority which must be shown on the main river map of the authority.

The **Rivers Pollution Prevention Acts, 1976 and 1893** (later repealed and replaced by the Rivers (Prevention of Pollution) Acts, 1951-1961) used the term "stream", which was defined by s.20 of the 1876 Act to include "rivers, streams, canals, lakes and watercourses, other than watercourses at the time of the passing of the Act used mainly as sewers, and emptying directly into the sea or tidal waters". That term also included the sea to such extent, and tidal waters to such point, as, after local inquiry and on sanitary grounds, might be determined by order of the Local Government Board.

Now, by s 56(1) of the **Control of Pollution Act, 1974,** "stream" includes any river, watercourse or inland water whether natural or artificial or above or below ground, but does not include (*a*) any lake or pond not discharging to a stream; (*b*) any sewer vested in a water authority; or (c) any tidal waters. A reference to a stream includes a reference to the channel or bed of a stream which is for the time being dry.

Section 4 of the **Salmon and Freshwater Fisheries Act, 1975,** refers to waters containing fish and "tributaries thereof", and the meaning of "tributary" has been the subject of several decisions. The following have been held not to be tributaries — an artificial reservoir (*Stead* v. *Nicholas* (1901) 65 J.P. 484), indirect tributaries (*Merricks* v. *Cadwallader* (1881) 46 J.P.216, D.C.), a reservoir formed by a dam placed across a stream (*Harbottle* v. *Terry* (1882) 47 J.P.136) and a reservoir constructed across a river valley; *George* v. *Carpenter* (1893) 57 J.P.311.

The **Public Health Act, 1936,** makes several references to watercourses. Section 30 speaks of "any natural or artificial stream, watercourse, canal, pond or lake," and in ss.259-263 and 266 the terms "ditch," "watercourse," stream" are variously made use of. None of these expressions are defined by the Act and resource must be had to the common law interpretation. There have been quite a number of cases in which a stream, by reason of the discharge of sewage thereto, has been held to be a sewer, and this point was finally resolved in the House of Lords in *George Legge & Son, Ltd.* v. *Wenlock Corpn.* (1938) 102 J.P.93, which established that the status of a natural stream cannot be changed to that of a sewer within the meaning of the Public Health Act, 1875, by the discharge of sewage into it since the coming into operation of the Rivers Pollution Prevention Act, 1876.

The **River Boards Act, 1948,** (now repealed) referred to "rivers, streams and inland waters" without finding it necessary to define such. From the point of view of water authorities and the exercise of their various functions, *i.e.*, land drainage, pollution prevention, fisheries, water supply, sewerage and sewage disposal, the conservation of water and, occasionally, navigation, a comprehensive aspect is taken of rivers, embracing not only the river or group of rivers within the water authority area, but also the tributaries, streams and ditches which connect with the major watercourses, the catchment area and, where applicable, adjoining tidal waters. This is, however, subject to the qualification that land drainage functions are restricted to those watercourses shown as "main river" on the official map of the catchment or river board area, and powers relating to navigation are confined to navigable waters.

The **Water Resources Act, 1963,** s.135, gives possibly the widest definition to "inland water," which (within a water authority area) means (a) a river, stream, or other watercourse, whether natural or artificial and whether tidal or not; (b) a lake or pond, whether natural or artificial, and a reservoir or dock; and (c) a channel, creek, bay, estuary or arm of the sea. The same provision also defines "watercourse" as including all rivers, streams, ditches, drains, cuts, culverts, dykes, sluices, sewers and passages through which water flows, except (1) mains and water fittings, (2) water authority sewers, and (3) adits or passages used in connection with wells and boreholes. These two definitions from the Water Resources Act, 1963, have also been applied to the **Water Act, 1973** (see s.38 thereof).

RIPARIAN RIGHTS

Occupiers of land immediately bordering a river derive, through their actual possession of such land, rights at common law both in quantity and purity. Whilst statute law has affected these rights, the common law still provides formidable remedies for any breach of the rights.

It is the writer's experience that many people regard riparian rights, or "water rights," with some suspicion and doubt, deserving of an opinion of counsel before any dealings with such rights are begun. It is hoped here to shed a little light on an interesting topic, and an important part of the law relating to waters and watercourses.

The owner or occupier of land abutting on a stream, or through which a river flows, is entitled to the enjoyment of certain "riparian" rights. For riparian rights properly so named to arise, the land must be in actual contact with the stream, laterally or vertically, and there is no distinction in principle between riparian rights on the banks of navigable or tidal rivers and on those of non-navigable rivers: *North Shore Railway* v. *Pion* (1889) 61 L.T. 525, P.C.

The rights which a riparian proprietor has with respect to the water are entirely derived from the possession of land abutting on the river, and if he grants away any portion of the land so abutting the grantee becomes a riparian proprietor and has similar rights. If he grants away part of his estate not abutting on the river, the grantee has no water rights by virtue merely of his occupation: *Stockport Waterworks Co.* v. *Potter* (1864) 10 L.T. 748. Riparian rights are founded on the right of access to the stream and a riparian tenement must be in reasonable proximity to the water; a site some distance from a river but connected to it by a strip of land may be too far from the river bank to sustain the character of a riparian tenement: *Attwood* v. *Llay Main Collieries* (1926) 134 L.T. 268. The right to have a stream to flow in its natural state without diminution or alteration is an incident to the property in the land through which it passes: *Embrey* v. *Owen* (1851) 6 Ex. 353.

In dealing with riparian rights it is convenient to distinguish between those which concern the bed and banks of a water course and those which relate to the use and flow of the running stream.

Rights concerning the bed and banks

In *Bickett* v. *Morris* (1866) 30 J.P. 532, it was held that each proprietor on the banks of a non-tidal river has a property in the soil of the *alveus* (bed) from his own side to the *medium filum fluminis*, but is not entitled to use the *alveus* in such a manner as to interfere with the natural flow of the water or abridge the width of the stream, or to interfere with its natural course, but anything done *in alveo* which produces no sensible effect on the stream is allowable. A riparian owner on the banks of a tidal river has no greater rights to use the *alveus* than he has on a non-tidal river: *A.-G.* v. *Lonsdale* (1868) 20 L.T. 64.

A riparian owner may place stakes and wattles on the soil of a river to prevent erosion by floods and make pens in the stream to prevent cattle from straying: *Hanbury* v. *Jenkins* (1901) 65 J.P. 631. He is entitled to raise his banks to protect his property from flooding, so long as he conducts his operations so as not to do any actual injury to property on the other side of the river: *Bickett* v. *Morris, supra*. As regards fishing, the presumption is that the owner of the bed of a non-tidal river has the right to fish in the stream and to prevent other persons from fishing there: *Blount* v. *Layard* [1891] 2 Ch. 681.

It should be noted that a riparian or sea frontager is not at common law under a liability to maintain his frontage for the protection of adjoining land owners (*Hudson* v. *Tabor* (1877) 42 J.P. 20), apart from any obligation which may be imposed upon him by covenant, statute, prescription, etc. Nor is a riparian owner required to clear the channel if it becomes silted up and choked with weeds (*Hodgson* v. *York Corporation* (1873) 37 J.P. 725, and he may not remove a natural accretion of gravel or shoal on the bed of a river so as to restore the flow of the water to its former state as regards velocity, direction, and height: *Withers* v. *Purchase* (1889) 60 L.T. 819.

These common law rules must, however, be construed in the light of The Land Drainage Act, 1976, which, *inter alia*, provides that watercourses must be put in proper order if the condition of the stream is likely to impede the proper flow of the water (s.18); enables obligations to repair watercourses and drainage works to be enforced (s.24), and requires that the erection of dams, weirs, and other like obstructions in watercourses and the erection or alteration of structures across watercourses must be approved by the appropriate drainage authority (ss.28 and 29). Further provisions are to be found in the land drainage bye-laws of these authorities and in subsequent legislation, *e.g.*, ss.263 *et seq.*, of the Public Health Act, 1936.

Rights on navigable rivers

A riparian owner on the banks of a tidal navigable river has rights and natural easements similar to those which belong to a riparian owner above the flow of the tide, subject to the public right of navigation: *Lyon* v. *Fishmongers' Co.* (1876) 42 J.P. 163. Generally speaking, a land owner may make such use of the bed of the river as he thinks fit, provided the public right of navigation is not interfered with: *Orr Ewing* v. *Colquhoun* (1877) 2 A.C. 839. Any works erected on the bed of a navigable river may, owing to a change in the bed or other circumstances, become at future time a nuisance and liable to abatement: *A.-G.* v. *Terry* (1874) 38 J.P. 340.

The rights on navigable rivers relate mainly to mooring and access. A riparian owner is entitled to moor vessels of ordinary size at a wharf alongside his property for the purposes of loading and unloading at reasonable times and for a reasonable period, and it does not matter if the vessel overlaps his premises, provided it does not interfere with the proper right of access to neighbouring premises, if used as a dock by vessels: *Original Hartlepool Collieries* v. *Gibb* (1877) 41 J.P. 660. A riparian proprietor may construct and moor a floating wharf and boathouse off his premises provided it does not obstruct the navigation (*Booth* v. *Ratte* (1889) 62 L.T. 198), and it might be mentioned here that the mooring of houseboats in a navigable channel, as distinct from the construction of landing stages and other associated works, does not require planning permission: (1951) J.P.L. 665. On a non-navigable river, a riparian owner might perhaps be able to establish a right to boat for purposes of recreation for himself and his family by custom: *Bourke* v. *Davis* (1889) 62 L.T. 34.

A public navigable river is a public highway and the owners of land on the banks have a right to go on the river from any spot on their own land (*Marshall* v. *Ulleswater Steam Navigation Co.* (1871) 36 J.P. 583), and any interference with a right to access to a navigable river is actionable without proof of special damage: *Rose* v. *Groves* (1843) 5 M. & G. 613.

Natural rights relating to the flowing water are divisible into those concerned with the natural quantity of the water, *e.g.*, its diversion, obstruction and abstraction, and those concerned with the natural quality of the water, *i.e.*, its purity and pollution.

Natural rights in respect of quantity

The common law rights of the riparian owner to take water from the stream have, since 1st July, 1965, been restricted, in that, apart from being able to abstract water for his domestic household purposes and agricultural purposes other than spray irrigation (and the other relevant exceptions mentioned in s.24 of the Water Resources Act, 1963), he must hold a licence to abstract the water from the water authority in accordance with the provisions of the Water Resources Acts, 1963-1971.

A riparian owner has a right to the reasonable use of the water for

his domestic purposes and for his cattle, without regard to the effect
which that use may have in case of a deficiency of water upon proprietors lower down the stream. He also has a right to the use of the water
for any purpose, or what may be deemed the extraordinary use of it,
provided he does not thereby interfere with the rights of other proper-
etors either above or below him: *Miner* v. *Gilmour* (1859) 12 Moo.
P.C. 156. This also holds good as regards tidal rivers: *Lyon* v. *Fishmongers' Co., supra.*

"Domestic purposes" extend to culinary purposes, to purposes of
cleansing and washing, feeding and supplying the ordinary quantities
of cattle and so on: *A.-G.* v. *Great Eastern Railway Co.* (1871) 35 J.P.
788. An "extraordinary use" includes purposes of manufacture (*Dakin*
v. *Cornish* (1845) 6 Ex. 360), diversion of a watercourse for irrigation
so long as the running stream is not exhausted (*Embrey* v. *Owen, supra*),
or the damming of a river in connexion with a mill: *Belfast Ropeworks*
v. *Boyd* (1881) 21 L.R. Ir. 560. An extraordinary use to be exercised
lawfully must be a reasonable user and the purposes for which the
water are taken must be connected with the riparian tenement:
Swindon Waterworks Co. v. *Wilts. and Berks. Canal Co.* (1875) 40 J.P.
804, where it was held that the right of riparian owners to collect water
from a stream into a permanent reservoir to supply an adjoining town
was not a reasonable use of the water. In *McCartney* v. *Londonderry Co.*
[1904] A.C. 301, the court decided that a railway company whose line
crossed a river were not entitled to collect water from the river for
working their locomotives, this not being a purpose connected with the
land where it crossed the stream.

A riparian owner may use the water of a stream for purposes of
irrigation so long as he returns the water to the stream diminished no
more than is inevitable by absorption and evaporation (*Embrey* v. *Owen,
supra*); but he must not delay the passage of the water so as to injure
the natural rights of a lower riparian owner: *Sampson* v. *Hoddinott*
(1857) 21 J.P. 375. The common law does not recognise ordinary or
extraordinary rights to take water for spray irrigation, since the water is
not returned to the river (*Rugby Joint Water Board* v. *Walters* [1966]
3 All E.R. 497).

These principles regulate the rights of land owners in respect of water
flowing in known and defined channels, whether upon or below the surface of the ground, but have no application to underground water
which merely percolates through the strata in no known channels:
Chasemore v. *Richards* (1859) 23 J.P. 596. Whether the same principles
apply to artificial channels depends (*a*) on the character of the watercourse, such as if it is temporary or permanent; (*b*) the circumstances
under which it was presumably created, and (*c*) the mode in which it
has been used and enjoyed: *Bailey & Co.* v. *Clark Son, & Morland*
(1902) 86 L.T. 309.

water prejudicial to the riparian owner, gives use to an action for damages and may be restrained by an injunction: *Sampson* v. *Hoddinott* (1857) I.C.B.N.S. 590.

Pollution and natural rights of purity

A riparian owner has a natural right to the flow of the stream past his land without sensible alteration in its character or quality. (*Young & Co.* v. *Bankier Distillery Co.* (1893) 58 J.P. 100), and the water must not be contaminated by trade waste discharged into the stream by a factory (*Crossley* v. *Lightowler* (1867) 16 L.T. 438) or by sewage from a town: *Jones* v. *Llanrwst U.D.C.* (1911) 75 J.P. 68: *cp*. also the post-war cases of injunction, such as *Pride of Derby Angling Association, Ltd.* v. *British Celanese, Ltd.* [1953] 1 All E.R. 179; 117 J.P. 52. This rule also applies to underground water (*Hodgkinson* v. *Ennor (1863)* 27 J.P. 469) and to artificial watercourses which are of a permanent nature or in respect of which riparian rights have been acquired: *Sutcliffe* v. *Booth* (1863) 27 J.P. 613. Pollution is, in itself, an unlawful act and a nuisance, and differs from the obstruction or diversion of a stream, which when done in a reasonable manner and on the person's own property is a lawful use of property: *Hodgkinson* v. *Ennor, supra.*

It is no answer for a defendant to show that the water which he has polluted is also polluted by other persons (*St. Helen's Smelting Co.* v. *Tipping* (1865) 29 J.P. 579), and where an injury has been done to a private person's rights, he is entitled to damages, even nominal damages, and where an injury is apprehended an injunction will be granted against the person in default: *Nixon* v. *Tynemouth Union* (1888) 52 J.P. 504, D.C. Pollution which causes annoyance to the public in general is a public nuisance , and the person responsible may be indicted for a misdemeanour (*R.* v. *Bradford Navigation Co.* (1865) 29 J.P. 613), or an injunction applied for by the Attorney-General: *A.-G.* v. *Shrewsbury Bridge Co.* (1882) 46 L.T. 687.

The pollution of water has been the subject of many statutes, both local and general, designed to prohibit or restrict pollution, including the Rivers (Prevention of Pollution) Acts, 1951-1961, the Control of Pollution Act, 1974, (concerned with river pollution), part II of the Public Health Act, 1936 (sewage disposal), the Public Health (Drainage of Trade Premises) Act, 1937 (disposal of trade wastes), and a host of miscellaneous legislation ranging from fisheries and the protection of water supplies to diseased animal carcasses and atomic waste.

So far, natural riparian rights have been discussed, but natural rights of water may be altered or enlarged, when they are known as acquired rights or easements.

Acquired rights (Easements of water)

A riparian owner may by usage acquire a right to use the water in a manner not justified by his natural rights, but the acquired right has no operation against the natural rights of another riparian proprietor, unless the use by which it was acquired affects the use that the land owner has of the stream, or his power to use it, so as to raise the presumption of a grant and so render the tenement above or below a servient tenement: *Sampson* v. *Hoddinott, supra.* Examples of prescriptive rights are the right to go on a neighbour's land to open lock gates or to repair the banks or to dam back water. An easement may be acquired to obstruct and divert the waters of a stream, *e.g.*, the use of a mill water-wheel which requires a dam or mill-head to pen back the water (*Saunders* v. *Newman* (1818) 1 B. & A. 258), so long as the diversion or obstruction is not materially altered or increased to the detriment of the servient owner: *Bealey* v. *Shaw* (1805) 6 East. 208. Easements of water may arise by express or implied grant, by devise, under custom or statute, or by prescription either at common law or under the Prescription Act, 1832.

An easement may also be acquired to pollute the waters of a stream, as, for instance, the claim by custom or prescription to use a stream for washing ore and carrying away rubble discharged in working a mine (*Carlyon* v. *Lovering* (1857) 1 H. & N. 797), or discharging polluted water: (*Wright* v. *Williams* (1836) 1 M. & W. 77.) But such a right can only be gained by a continuous and perceptible amount of injury to the servient tenement for 20 years (*Murgatroyd* v. *Robinson* (1857) 7 E. & B. 391) and once a right to pollute has been acquired the fouling must not be appraciably increased to the detriment of the servient tenement: *M'Intyre Brothers* v. *M'Gavin* [1893] A.C. 268. There can be no prescriptive right to pollute waters in contravention of a statute, thus a prescriptive right to foul a stream cannot be acquired after the coming into operation of the Rivers Pollution Prevention Act, 1876 (*Butterworth* v. *West Riding of Yorkshire Rivers Board* (1909) 73 J.P. 89), or perhaps after the Local Government Act (1858) Amendment Act, 1861: *Legge & Sons, Ltd.* v. *Wenlock Corporation* [1938] 1 All E.R. 37: 102 J.P.93.

NAVIGABLE RIVERS

A river has many functions and uses, some are exercised when water is abstracted or diverted from the channel, and some are exercised within the confines of the banks, such as fishing and recreation; where a right of navigation exists, the use of the river as a highway ranks high.

There are two types of navigable river: tidal navigable rivers, and inland rivers where a right of navigation exists. Canals, as artificial waterways constructed solely for purposes of navigation, are creatures of statute and are not discussed here.

A navigable river is a public highway navigable by all Her Majesty's subjects in a reasonable manner and for a reasonable purpose (*Original Hartlepool Collieries Co.* v. *Gibb* (1877) 41 J.P. 660), and at common law the public have always had a right, paramount to any power in the Crown, to navigate over every part of a common navigable river: *Williams* v. *Wilcox* (1838) 8 Ad. & El. 314. The right of navigation is simply a right of way, and the public have a mere right to use the river for the purposes of navigation similar to the right the public have to pass along a public road or footpath through a private estate. The public who have acquired by use the right to navigate on an inland water have no right of property (*Orr Ewing* v. *Colquhoun* (1877) 2 App. Cas. 839), and commissioners appointed by statute to make navigable a natural river do not thereby have the bed of the river vested in them, but have a mere easement (*R.* v. *Aire & Calder Navigation Co.* (1829) 9 B. & C. 820); nor do the proprietors of a navigation necessarily acquire an interest in the soil of the banks which would enable them to maintain an action for trespass: *Hollis* v. *Goldfinch* (1823) 1 B. & C. 205. A public right of navigation is not a public right of way for the purposes of the National Parks etc. Act, 1949, s.20 and byelaws thereunder (*Evans* v. *Godbee* [1974] 3 All E.R. 341),

The right of navigation in tidal waters is a right of way thereover for all the public purposes of navigation, trade, and intercourse (*Blundell* v. *Catterall* (1821) 5 B. & Ald. 268), and the right of passage on a pub-

13

lic navigable river is not suspended when the tide is too low for vessels to float: *Colchester Corporation* v. *Brooke* (1845) 7 Q.B. 339.

Whether a particular water is navigable depends upon the situation and nature of the channel and not every ditch or cutting forms part of the public navigable river, though it is large enough to admit the passage of a boat. A tidal creek, formed by the water of a tidal river filling excavations made owing to clay dug from land adjoining the river and formerly dry, was used by boats in connexion with the working of the clay. There was no evidence that the creek was used by the public as a waterway, nor was it likely to be so used. The court decided that the creek was not part of a public navigable river: *Sim E. Bak* v. *Ang Yong Huat* [1923] A.C. 429. Every creek or river into which the tide flows is not on that account necessarily a public navigable channel, although sufficiently large for that purpose: *R.* v. *Montague* (1825) 4 B. & C. 598.

A tidal navigable river means a river which is subject to the vertical flow and reflow of the ordinary tides and navigable as such. It includes the navigable parts of the river where the fresh water is arrested by the horizontal flow of the tide. Portions of a river which are affected only by extraordinary high tides are not part of the navigable river: *Reece* v. *Miller* (1882) 47; *West Riding of Yorkshire Rivers Board* v. *Tadcaster R.D.C.* (1882) 8 Q.B.D. 626. The flowing of the ordinary tides is strong *prima facie* evidence of the existence of a public navigable river (*Rose* v. *Miles* (1814) 5 Taunt. 705), but whether a river is navigable or not is a question for a jury: *Vooght* v. *Winch* (1819) 2 B. & Ald. 662. It is a question of evidence of the ebb and flow whether the waters are tidal (*Ingram* v. *Percival* [1969] 1 Q.B. 548). The rights of the public over tidal navigable rivers are usually confined to navigation and fishing, and the right of navigation must be exercised reasonably, and where it conflicts with a right of fishing the right must not be abused so as to work an inquiry to the right of fishing: *Original Hartlepool Colleries Co.* v. *Gibb, supra.*

The public have no general right to navigate non-tidal waters, the soil of which *prima facie* belongs to the riparian owners, but the right may arise from dedication, immemorial usage, statute or by grant from the riparian owner. In the case of *Bourke* v. *Davis* (1889) 62 L.T. 34, the defendant claimed a right of way for boats on the River Mole, a non-tidal tributary of the Thames, and sought to restrain the plaintiff, a riparian owner, from obstructing the Mole with posts and chains, where that river passed through his lands. The evidence showed that the reach in question could not be approached from below by boats, that its depth was artificial and depended on mill-dams, that it had never been used for commerce or as a way from one public place to another, that there was no public access to it at one end and that it was doubtful whether there was any public access to it for boats at any points. No maintenance had been carried out on the Mole, except occasional dredging by mill-owners. There had been a good deal of boating on the reach by riparian owners and others in boats brought from a distance, mainly for fishing, but no right to fish was claimed. The court decided that the use had been permissive and not of right, and the defendant's claim failed.

A right to navigate on private waters is confined to the extent of the grant or user provided, unlike the public right of navigation on tidal waters, which is unlimited at all times for all types of vessels and extends to all parts of the channel. The right to navigate on non-tidal waters includes boating for pleasure, although the mere existence of such a right or custom by itself does not establish a public right (*Bourke* v. *Davis, supra*), but does not include the right to fish (*Smith* v. *Andrews* (1891) 2 Ch. 678) or to shoot wildfowl: *Micklethwait* v. *Vincent* (1892) 67 L.T. 225. Since the banks of non-tidal rivers belong to the riparian owners, the right of navigation does not include the right to moor at, land on, or tow along the banks, although such rights can be acquired by custom, prescription, dedication, or statute. A right for the public to embark or disembark on private ground or to beach or move vessels there for carrying or a boat hirer's business cannot be acquired by prescription (*Leith-Buchanan* v. *Hogg* [1931] S.C. 204). Whether a particular place on the bank of a river exists as a public landing place for all the King's subjects depends upon the evidence that may be available: *Drinkwater* v. *Porter* (1835) 7 C. & P. 181, N.P.

The term "navigable" contains within it all such rights upon the waterway as, with relation to the circumstances of each river, are necessary for the full and convenient passage of vessels and boats along the channel: it does not interfere with the rights of individuals along the banks. A vessel may remain aground until the tide serves, and no toll can be demanded by the proprietor of the soil therefor: *Colchester Corporation* v. *Brooke, supra*. The riparian owner on a navigable river holds possession of the soil subject to the rights of all persons navigating the river to use the waters in all ordinary navigable ways and the rights of the owners of vessels to fix moorings in the soil, for the purpose of attaching their vessels to them, may be claimed by immemorial user, grant, or as a concession: *A.-G.* v. *Wright* [1897] 2 Q.B. 318. The right to anchor either by means of an anchor or mooring is a necessary part of the right to navigate in tidal waters (*Gann* v. *Free Fishers of Whitstable* (1865) 29 J.P. 243), but there is no common law right to lay permanent moorings on another person's property without his permission and it is not an ordinary right of navigation, although such a right may arise by custom or statute (*Fowey Marine (Emsworth) Ltd.* v. *Gafford* [1968] 1 All E.R. 979). A vessel is entitled to remain in a place until the wind or the weather, or probably also the season, permit it to leave, or until it has obtained a cargo or completed repairs: *Den-*

aby & Cadeby Main Collieries, Ltd. v. *Anson* [1911] 1 K.B. 171.
    If the course of a navigable river is altered it seems that the right of
navigation follows the new channel (*Mayor of Carlisle* v. *Graham*
(1869) L.R. 4 Ex. 366), and the right of navigation is restored to the
new cut where navigation commissioners restore a silted up navigable
channel: *R.* v. *Betts* (1850) 16 Q.B. 1022. A public right of navigation
in a river or creek may be extinguished either by Act of Parliament,
writ of *ad quod damnum*, or inquisition thereon, or under certain circumstances by commissioners of sewers (now water authorities), or by
natural causes, such as the recess of the sea or an accumulation of mud,
etc.: *R.* v. *Montague, supra.*

THE PUBLIC AND THE FORESHORE

That part of the seashore between high and low water marks is often commonly supposed to be open to all for any or many purposes. Legally, though, its use is confined to navigation and fishing for the public.

Each summer many of the public migrate to the seaside bent on leisure and recreation, and may spend some time on the seashore. It would be rather much to expect that any of this community, whilst in holiday mood, would have the inclination to consider what rights he has at law to use and enjoy the seashore; but let it be supposed that a lawyer on vacation (for want of something better to do on a rainy day) does find time to reflect upon the rights of the individual at large in relation to the seashore.

First of all, what is meant by the term "seashore"? The seashore, or "foreshore," as it is commonly called — the two words meaning the same in the strict legal sense (*Mellor* v. *Walmesley* (1905) 93 L.T. 574) — is the land between the high and low water marks at ordinary tides, that is to say, between the ordinary flux and reflux of the sea: *Blundell* v. *Catterall* (1821) 5 B & Ald. 268. "Sea beach" has the same meaning as seashore (*Government of State of Penang* v. *Beng Hong Oou* [1971] 3 All E.R. 1163). An ordinary high tide is taken at the point of the line of the medium high tide between the springs and neaps, ascertained by taking the average of the medium tides during the year: *Tracey Elliot* v. *Morley (Earl)* (1907) 51 S.J. 625. The foreshore in the public mind is, perhaps, associated with the waste part of the beach or sands beyond the promenade or highway which usually exists in built-up seaside areas, or, in places more remote, the beach situate beyond visible boundary walls or private property. But legally, the foreshore refers to that part which lies below high water mark of ordinary tides: *A.-G.* v. *Chambers* (1854) 18 J.P. 583. Land above the foreshore is presumed to belong to adjoining owners: *Lowe* v. *Govett* (1832) 1 L.J.K.b. 224.

Secondly, who owns the foreshore? *Prima facie*, the right to the soil between high and low water mark is vested in the Crown, unless the

17

Crown at some time or other has parted with it (*Le Strange* v. *Rowe* (1866) 4 F. & F. 1048), and there is no legal presumption that the sea-shore between high and low water mark belongs to the owner of the adjoining land: *Webber* v. *Richards* (1844) 2 L.T.O.S. 420. The Crown may have parted with the property in the soil of the foreshore to a subject; thus, the Crown may have granted the foreshore by letters patent to a town council (*A.-G.* v. *Burridge* (1822) 10 Price 350) or to the lord of a manor (*A.-G.* v. *Hammer* (1858) 22 J.P. 543), but the onus of proving an adverse title against the Crown rests on the defendant: *A.-G.* v. *Richards* (1795) 2 Anst. 603. A subject may acquire the foreshore from the Crown by charter, grant or by way of prescription. A grant by the Crown is subject to the rights of the public over the foreshore:*A.-G. Burridge, supra.* Evidence of acts of ownership and long usage are admissible in proof of a grant of foreshore: *Calmady* v. *Rowe* (1844) 6 C.B. 861.

Next to be considered are the rights or supposed rights which the public have at common law with respect to the foreshore, and these may be classified as follows: (1) navigation; (2) fishing; (3) passage; (4) taking seaweed and shells; (5) taking sand, gravel and shingle; (6) bathing; (7) wreck.

Navigation

The ownership of the Crown in the soil of the foreshore is subject to the public rights of navigation and fishing and rights ancillary thereto, and no grant of the foreshore by the Crown to a subject can operate to the detriment of the public right of fishing and that of navigation. The public have no rights over the foreshore when not covered by the tide, except such as are ancillary to these rights of fishing and navigation in the sea. When covered by the tide the foreshore is part of the sea, and the only rights of the public in or over it are the rights of navigation and fishing and rights ancillary thereto: *Fitzhardinge (Lord)* v. *Purcell* (1908) 72 J.P. 276.

The right of navigation belongs by law to all the subjects of the realm and the right to anchor is a necessary part of the right to navigate: *Gann* v. *Free Fishers of Whitstable* (1865) 29 J.P. 243. Whether navigation includes the right to ground on the shore depends on the circumstances of each case. If a vessel cannot reach her destination in a single tide it is reasonable for her to remain aground until the tide serves: *Colchester Corporation* v. *Brooke* (1845) 15 L.J.Q.B. 59. An immemorial user of the foreshore by the owners of fishing boats and other craft, by fixing moorings in the soil, for the purpose of attaching their boats to them, may be supported either as an ordinary incident of the navigation, or on a presumption of a legal origin by grant from the Crown of the foreshore subject to such user, or by concession by a former owner of the foreshore to all persons navigating the waters to use it for fixing moorings: *A.-G.* v. *Wright* (1879) 77 L.T. 295.

Fishing

The public have a right to fish between high and low water mark (*Mayor of Orford* v. *Richardson* (1791) 4 T.R. 473), subject to any statutory restrictions, such as the Sea Fisheries Regulation Act, 1966. Only the ordinary methods of fishing may be employed on the foreshore and fixed fishing engines or staked nets cannot be used: *Bevins* v. *Bird* (1865) 12 L.T. 306; *Olding* v. *Wild* (1866) 30 J.P. 295. The public right of fishing includes the right to take shell fish on the foreshore (*Goodman* v. *Saltash Corporation* (1882) 7 A.C. 633), but fishermen, save under exceptional circumstances, are not entitled to draw up or leave their boats above high water mark: *Ilchester* v. *Rashleigh* (1889) 5 T.L.R. 739. The public right of fishing is subservient to the right of navigation: *A.-G.* v. *Parmeter* (1811) 10 Price 378. The public cannot take royal fish, *i.e.*, whale, sturgeon, or porpoise, which when caught near the coast or thrown on the seashore belong to the Crown and not to the finder (17 Edw. 2 st. 7 c. 11). The right for fishermen inhabitants of a parish to spread their nets to dry on private land may be established as a valid custom: *Mercer* v. *Denne* (1905) 70 J.P. 65.

Passage

Subject to part V of the National Parks and Access to the Countryside Act, 1949, as amended by the Countryside Act, 1968, whereby the public may enjoy access for open air recreation to open country (which includes foreshore), there exists no right for the public to pass and repass over the foreshore for all purposes, and the public rights with respect to the sea and foreshore are rights upon the water, not upon the land of passage and fishing on the sea and foreshore when covered with water. In exercise of these rights the public must have the means of getting to and upon the water for such purposes, but only by and from such places as usage or necessity have appropriated to these purposes, and there is no general right of lading, unloading, landing and embarking where the public please upon the sea, shore or the land adjoining thereto. But the public may use the foreshore generally in cases of peril or necessity, *e.g.*, shipwreck: *Blundell* v. *Catterall, supra; Brinckman* v. *Matley* (1904) 68 J.P. 534, and *see* s.513 of the Merchant Shipping Act 1894. The public's right to enter upon the foreshore is limited to the purpose of navigation or fishing: *Llandudno U.D.C.* v. *Woods* (1899) 63 J.P. 775. The owner of the foreshore may bring an action for an injunction to restrain trespass. *Behrens* v. *Richards* (1905) 69 J.P. 381.

Similarly, the public have no right at common law to hold meetings on the foreshore, without the consent of the owner (*Brighton Corporation* v. *Packham* (1908) 72 J.P. 318), nor for a clergyman to conduct religious services there: *Llandudno U.D.C.* v. *Woods, supra.* A right to place chairs on the foreshore for hire cannot be claimed by prescription under the Prescription Act, 1832: *Ramsgate Corporation* v. *Debling* (1906) 70 J.P. 132.

An owner or occupier of land adjoining the sea has the same right of access to the sea as a riparian proprietor has in respect of a tidal river (*A.-G. of Straits Settlement* v. *Wemyss* (1888) 13 A.C. 192), and when the tide is out this right includes a right of access to the sea across the uncovered foreshore: *Coppinger* v. *Sheeham* [1906] 1 I.R. 519.

Taking seaweed and shells

The public are entitled to take floating seaweed as an incident of the right to navigate or fish (*Baird* v. *Fortune* (1861) 25 J.P. 691), but not seaweed cast or growing on the foreshore, since such is the property of the owner of the foreshore (*Howe* v. *Stawell* (1883) Alc. & N. 348), who may bring an action in trover or trespass for the wrongful taking of seaweed cast by the sea on the foreshore: *Brew* v. *Haren* (1877) L.R. 11 C.L. 198. The lord of a manor cannot, except by grant or prescription, establish a claim to the exclusive right to cut seaweed on rocks below low water mark: *Benest* v. *Pipon* (1829) 1 Knapp 60.

There is some doubt whether the public can take fish shells found on the seashore between high and low water marks. On the one hand, the public have a right to take fish found on the foreshore (*Bagott* v. *Orr* (1801) 2 Bos. & P. 472); on the other hand, shells found or washed up on the foreshore belong to the owner of the foreshore as natural products of the shore.

Taking sand, gravel and shingle

Sand, shingle and gravel on the foreshore can only be removed by the owner of the foreshore, not by the general public (*Howe* v. *Stawell, supra*), except under the title of a statute, *e.g. see* 7 Jac. 1 c. 18 (1609), or by prescription. A claim to take shingle, etc., by the inhabitants of a township founded on custom is bad, since the claim relates to a profit *a prendre* which can only exist in grant or prescription: *Constable* v. *Nicholson* (1863) 14 C.B.N.S. 230. A fluctating body such as the inhabitants of a country cannot acquire a prescriptive right to take sea-washed coal from the foreshore (*Alfred F. Beckett Ltd.* v. *Lyons* [1966] Ch. 449). An injunction may be applied for against taking valuable stones found within the limits of the foreshore (*Cowper (Earl)* v. *Baker* (1890) 17 Ves. 128) and a claim cannot extend to removing shingle from the foreshore so as to destroy a natural barrier and expose land to the inroads of the sea: *A.-G* v. *Tomline* (1880) 44 J.P. 617. It is an offence under s.18 of the Coast Protection Act, 1949, to excavate or remove any materials (including minerals and turf) on, under, or forming part of the seashore to which that section applies, except under licence from a coast protection authority and an order under s.18 forbidding the extraction of gravel save under licence may be drafted wide enough to protect the seashore from whatever cause (*British Dredging (Services) Ltd.* v. *Secretary of State for Wales* (1974), *Times,* 3rd December). As to the powers of highway authorities to take materials for the maintenance or repair of highways from sea beaches, *see* ss. 48, 55, of the Highways Act, 1959.

Bathing

The public have no right at common law to bathe in the sea, nor any right to cross the seashore on foot, or with bathing machines, for that purpose; but the inhabitants of a vill or parish may by custom or prescription gain a right to use the foreshore for bathing: *Blundell* v. *Catterall, supra; Llandudno U.D.C.* v. *Woods, supra.* It makes no difference whether the foreshore is the property of the Crown or of a private owner: *Brinckman* v. *Matley* (1904) 68 J.P. 534. The regulation by a local authority of bathing in the sea may be effected either under a private Act or by byelaws made under s.82 of the Public Health Acts Amendment Act, 1907 or s.231 of the Public Health Act, 1936, as amended by s.17 of the Local Government (Miscellaneous Provisions) Act, 1976.

Shooting

The public have no right to kill and carry away wild fowl on the foreshore either when the foreshore is covered by the tide or uncovered, but where the foreshore is owned by a subject he is entitled to shoot thereon: *Fitzhardinge (Lord)* v. *Purcell* (1908) 72 J.P. 276.

Wreck

The right to unclaimed wreck found on the shore in any part of Her Majesty's dominions belongs to the Crown, except where the right has been granted to other persons: Merchant Shipping Act, 1894, s.523. The Court of Admiralty has jurisdiction over wreck between high and low water mark when the tide is high, and the courts of common law when the tide is low: *R.* v. *Two Casks of Tallow* (1837) 3 Hagg. 294. Wreck may consist of a ship or part of a ship or her cargo which has been cast ashore and not claimed by the owner. Before such articles are cast ashore they are either jetsam, flotsam, lagan or derelict and are Admiralty droits, belonging to the Crown: *R.* v. 49 *Casks of Brandy* (1836) 3 Hagg. 257. Persons who render services in preserving wreck are entitled to make salvage claims; Merchant Shipping Act, 1894, s.546.

Administration of the foreshore

At common law the foreshore forms part of the body of the adjoining county, the justices of which, and not the Admiralty, have jurisdiction to take cognizance of offences committed there, whether the foreshore is covered with water or not (*Embleton* v. *Brown* (1860) 3 E. & E. 234), but, in the absence of evidence, the foreshore does not form part of the adjoining parish, and is *prima facie* extra-parochial: *R.* v. *Musson* (1858) 22 J.P. 609. Now, however, s 72 of the Local Government Act, 1972 provides that every accretion from the sea, whether natural or artificial, and any part of the seashore to the low water mark which did not on October 26, 1972 form part of a parish, is for all purposes of local government annexed to and incorporated with in England the parish or parishes which such accretion or seashore adjoins, and in Wales the community or communities which such accretion or seashore adjoins, in proportion to the extent of the common boundary, and is accordingly annexed to and incorporated with the district and county in which the parish or community is situate.

The management of the foreshore belonging to the Crown, and previously under the former Minister of Transport, is in the hands of the Crown Estate Commissioners. As distinct from the foreshore belonging to the Crown and vested in the Commissioners, the foreshore may form parcel of a manor or be vested in a local authority by purchase or lease from the Crown or the lord of the manor. Land adjoining the seashore if waste and undeveloped may be subject to rights of common: Law of Property Act, 1925, s.193.

Some maritime local authorities have obtained powers under local Acts to make byelaws and regulations as to sea beaches and foreshore vested in them; *see,* for instance, *Gray* v. *Sylvester* (1897) 61 J.P. 807; *Parker* v. *Bournemouth Corporation* (1902) 66 J.P. 440; *Moorman* v. *Tordoff* (1908) 72 J.P. 142; *Slee* v. *Meadows* (1911) 75 J.P. 142. Apart from this, where the district council own the foreshore, byelaws may be made either under s.164 of the Public Health Act, 1875, or s.15 of the Open Spaces Ace, 1906. Where ss.82 and 83 of the Public Health Acts Amendment Act, 1907, are in force a local authority may make byelaws for the regulation, etc., of the seashore. Byelaws as to navigation, speed and noise regarding pleasure boats propelled by internal combustion engines may be made under s.76 of the Public Health Act, 1961, and s.17 of the Local Government (Miscellaneous Provisions) Act, 1976.

RIVER BANKS AND SEA WALLS

It has been said that a river consists of the bed, its banks and the water flowing therein. Besides defining the course and limits of a watercourse, the banks are the backbone of any system of sea defence or flood prevention.

The term "bank" in connexion with a river does not appear to have been defined specifically by the English courts, although this was stated in *Monmouthshire Canal & Railway Co.* v. *Hill* (1859) 28 L.J. Ex. 283, as regards the banks of a canal — "When you speak of the banks of a canal, you mean the land on either side of the canal which confine the water. There are banks of the canal therefore on both sides of it, and when you speak of the banks you mean the substantial soil which confines the water." The same case decided that the banks of a canal include the towpath. In the American case of *Howard* v. *Ingersoll* (1851) 17 Ala 780, it was said with respect to fresh-water river banks that "banks are the elevations of land which confine the waters in their natural channel when they rise the highest and do not overflow the banks; and in that condition of the water the banks and the soil which is permanently submerged form the bed of the river. The banks are part of the river bed, but the river does not include beyond the banks. Fresh rivers, although not subject to the daily fluctuation of the tide, may rise and fall periodically at certain seasons and thus have defined high and low water marks."

In the case of *Jones* v. *Mersey River Board* [1957] 3 All E.R. 375 the court substantially adopted the definitions stated in the Monmouth and Ingersoll cases and went on to state that "bank" was not limited to the actual slope or vertical face where those banks met the river, but included the land adjoining or near to the river to the extent to which it served the river. See also *Oakes* v.*Mersey River Board* (1957) J.P.L.824.

Section 116 of the Land Drainage Act, 1976, defines "banks" as meaning "banks, walls or embankments adjoining or confining, or constructed for the purposes of or in connexion with, any channel or sea

front, and includes all land between the bank and low-water mark,"
but that definition does not include an artificial bank up to three-
quarters of a mile from the channel of a river: *North Level Commissioners*
v. *Welland Catchment Board* [1938] Ch. 379. A distinction was made
between river banks and walls in *Newcastle (Duke)* v. *Clark* (1818) 8
Taunt 627, to the effect that a bank belongs to the owner of the adjoining land, but that a wall is the property of the person bound to repair it.

As a general rule, the ownership and property in a river bank is
vested in the riparian owner, and the right to the bed of a river is not
inseparably bound up with the right to the bank, since an owner of
both may retain one and part with the other: *Smith* v. *Andrews* (1891)
65 L.T. 175. Where a company, body of commissioners or board of
conservators have been established by statute to carry on and regulate
the navigation of a river they do not necessarily acquire an interest in
the soil of the bank, unless this is required for the purposes of navigation: *Hollis* v. *Goldfinch* (1823) 1 B. & C. 205. It depends upon the construction of the Act as to whether the undertakers acquire an interest
or easement in the soil of the bank: *Badger* v. *South Yorks Rly. & River
Dun Co.* (1858) 1 E. & E. 359. The public have no right at common law
to tow along the banks of a navigable river (*Ball* v. *Herbert* (1789) 3
Term. Rep. 253), but the right can arise by dedication, statute, custom
or usage.

Banks are associated with a non-tidal or fresh-water river, and in the
case of a tidal river or estuary it would be proper to refer to "shores"
instead of banks, and this introduces the subjects of coast protection
and sea walls.

Coast protection

Originally the Crown prerogative included a duty to protect the realm
against the inroads of the sea by maintaining the natural barriers against
it, or by raising artificial barriers, but this obligation cannot be enforced
by the subjects against the Crown: *Hudson* v. *Tabor* (1877) 42 J.P. 20.
The exercise of the royal prerogative was effected by means of commissions of sewers issued from time to time by the King and ultimately
regulated by statute, commencing with 6 Hen. 6 c. 5 (1427) and con-
tinuing with a series of Sewer Acts, then Land Drainage Acts, culminat-
ing in the Land Drainage Act, 1976. The powers of water authorities
to undertake sea defence works are referred to in s.116 of the 1976 Act,
where the definition of "drainage" includes "defence against water,"
which expression in turn includes "defence against sea water; and in
s.17 which deals with drainage works for defence against sea water or
tidal water.

Having introduced land drainage as an element in sea defence, it is
also necessary to point out that by the Coast Protection Act, 1949,

maritime district councils are coast protection authorities (with provision for establishing coast protection boards and joint committees) empowered to carry out works of construction, repair, improvement, etc., for protecting land against erosion or encroachment by the sea.

Scott, L.J., in *Symes* v. *Essex Rivers Catchment Board* (1937) 101 J.P. 179, stated that it was an express or implied principle of the former Land Drainage Act, 1930, that catchment boards (now water authorities) had two main objects: (1) to control the flow of inland waters, and (2) to keep out sea water from farm lands.

As distinct from sea defences erected by the Crown or a public authority, a person occupying land adjacent to the sea may erect such defences as are necessary for preserving his land, although such erections may render it necessary for his neighbours to do likewise: *R.* v. *Pagham (Sussex) Commissioners* (1828) 8 B. & C. 355. But *see* now s.16 of the Coast Protection Act, 1949, whereby coast protection works (other than maintenance or repair) require the consent of the coast protection authority. A person who, for the protection of his property upon the sea, places rocks and piles on the foreshore which belongs to his neighbour, may acquire an easement over his neighbour's land for protecting his property from the sea by means of the rocks and piles placed on the land: *Philpot* v. *Bath* (1905) 49 S.J. 618. A subject, who is the owner of the foreshore, will be restrained by injunction from removing a natural bank of shingle, although removed for sale in the ordinary and legitimate way, if by such removal the neighbouring land is thereby exposed to the inroads of the sea: *A.-G.* v. *Tomline* (1880) 44 J.P. 617.

Sea walls

There is a certain amount of common law regarding the functions of sea walls. In *Symes* v. *Essex Rivers Catchment Board, supra,* concerning an ancient sea wall originally erected either by the Crown or by commissioners of sewers to prevent the excursion of the sea into the land behind the wall, it was held that no one can acquire any right to interfere with the operation of a sea wall so as to prevent it operating as intended by the Crown when it was built and, in particular, an owner of land outside the sea wall had no right to send sea water through the wall on to the land lying within the wall or to make a breach in the wall which would expose the land on the landward side to the risk of such an event happening. The power of a water authority under the Land Drainage Act, 1976, *e.g.*, to keep in good repair a sea wall are permissive only and not imperative, and the powers do not require or direct a board to do such work: *Smith* v. *Cawdle Fen Commissioners* (1938) 82 S.J. 890; *East Suffolk Rivers Catchment Board* v. *Kent* (1941) 105 J.P. 129; *Gillett* v. *Kent Rivers Catchment Board* [1938] 4 All E.R. 810.

Those responsible for a sea wall are entitled to an injunction to restrain a person from removing shingle, etc., so as to expose the wall and the lands protected thereby to a greater risk of inundation of the sea: *Canvey Island Commissioners* v. *Preedy* (1922) 86 J.P. 21. It would no doubt be open to the Attorney-General to maintain an action on behalf of the public to restrain the commission of such an act: *A.-G.* v. *Shrewsbury Bridge Co.* (1882) 46 L.T. 687. *See* also s.18 of the Coast Protection Act, 1949, under which a coast protection authority may be order prohibit the excavation or removal of materials on, under or forming part of the seashore.

Sometimes a highway is incorporated with a sea wall and where the public have during living memory enjoyed a way along the top of a sea wall or embankment made to protect adjoining lands from the sea, a dedication of a public highway may be presumed so far as is not inconsistent with the purposes of the sea wall: *Greenwich Board of Works* v. *Maudslay* (1870) 35 J.P. 8. The authority responsible for the repair of a sea wall (but not in occupation of the wall) with a public footpath along the top are required to repair the wall so as to restrain the sea water and are under no duty to keep the footpath in repair, nor liable to members of the public injured by using the wall which collapses: *Hunwick* v. *Essex Rivers Catchment Board* (1952) 116 J.P. 217.

Repair of banks and walls

In *Hudson* v. *Tabor, supra*, both the parties were owners of land adjoining a creek communicating with the sea and had been long accustomed to repairing each his own sea wall and to raise it as the sea encroached. During a high tide the sea overflowed T's sea wall and damaged H's land. It was held that, in the absence of a prescriptive liability, T was not liable at common law to repair his sea wall for the benefit of H. Whilst this case concerns sea frontages as regards a sea wall, it would appear in the light of that decision and the other cases hereafter mentioned, that the principle that there is no liability to repair at common law in the absence of evidence to the contrary, may be extended to riparian owners in relation to the banks of a river, whether tidal or not.

The rule in *Hudson* v. *Tabor* is liable to departure in cases where the frontager or owner is under an obligation to repair. Formerly, liabilities to repair arose under the following heads — frontage, ownership, prescription, custom, tenure, covenant and *usus rei* (Callis on *The Law of Sewers* (1622) pp. 115-122), but since *Hudson* v. *Tabor*, the grounds of frontage, ownership and *per usum rei* are not relevant, and only the remaining grounds have to be considered.

A sea frontager may be under a prescriptive liability to repair a sea wall and when the wall, although in sufficient repair to resist the flow of ordinary tides and the force of ordinary winds, is destroyed by extraordinary storm and high tide, it has to be determined on the evidence whether the frontager was bound to provide against the effects of ordinary tempest only or of extraordinary ones also: *R.* v. *Leigh* (1839) 10

Ad. & El. 398. If the evidence is that a frontager's prescriptive liability does not extend to the repair of damage due to extraordinary violence of the sea, the liability to repair the damage falls on all the owners in the level: *Fobbing Sewers Commissioners* v. *R.* (1886) 51 J.P. 227.

Where a corporation are liable to repair sea walls under a grant from the Crown, an individual who suffers damage in consequence of the neglect of the corporation to repair the walls may sue the corporation for damages: *Lyme Regis Corporation* v. *Henley* (1834) 1 Scott 29. For example of liabilities to repair a wall arising by reason of tenure, *see London & N.W. Railway* v. *Fobbing Levels Commission* (1896) 75 L.T. 629: *R.* v. *Baker* (1867) 31 J.P. 692, and under covenant *see Morland* v. *Cook* (1868) 18 L.T. 496. Sometimes the obligation is that a frontager must keep a sea wall at a certain height and failure to do so will render him liable to an action for negligence, and an act of God, such as an extraordinary high tide, will not excuse him: *Nitro-Phosphate Co.* v. *London Docks* (1878) 39 L.T. 433.

Obligation to repair may also be imposed by statute, *e.g.*, s.24 of the Land Drainage Act, 1976; s.106 of the Thames Conservancy Act, 1932; ss.262, 264 of the Public Health Act, 1936. Conservancy commissioners under a statutory obligation to maintain and repair a sea wall were held liable, not only for damage caused by the river overflowing reclaimed lands, but also for damage caused to land beyond the reclaimed lands by reason of the sea wall being insufficient in height to prevent the river overflowing: *Bramlett* v. *Tees Conservancy Commissioners* (1885) 49 J.P. 214. But a river authority responsible for the maintenance of navigation were held not to be liable to maintain flood banks set back behind the natural river banks since the banks were not constructed to confine the water within the bed of the river: *Vyner* v. *N.E. Railway* (1904) 20 T.L.R. 192.

The passing of the former Land Drainage Act, 1930, made no difference to the liability of obligations to repair banks and walls; s.26 (1) of that Act (now s.24 (1) of the Land Drainage Act, 1976) preserved existing liabilities, and *North Level Commissioners* v. *River Welland Catchment Board* (1938) 102 J.P. 82 decided that the general wording of the Act or any scheme made under it did not transfer an obligation to repair an artificial bank from the plaintiffs to the catchment board set up under the Act. Section 26 of the 1976 Act requires water authorities to commute all obligations imposed on persons "by reason of tenure, custom, prescription or otherwise" to, *inter alia*, repair banks of watercourses forming part of the board's "main river." The courts have decided that s.26 deals only with obligations which are referable to, charged on or arising out of some land and is not concerned with a purely contractual obligation (*Eton R.D.C.* v. *Thames Conservators* (1950) 114 J.P. 279), nor with a voluntary obligation arising under covenant: *Re Fitzherbert Brockhole's Agreement, River Wyre Catchment Board* v.

Miller (1939) 103 J.P. 379.

Finally, although he may be under no liability to repair a bank, an owner may be liable to abate a statutory nuisance due to flooding of his land by a breach in the bank *(Clayton* v. *Sale U.D.C.* (1926) 90 J.P. 5), and it is the common law duty of an owner to prevent his land from being so used as to be a public nuisance: *A.-G.* v. *Tod-Heatley* (1897) 76 L.T. 174. Conveyancers should take note of *Morland* v. *Cook, supra,* under which an intending purchaser of property situate below sea level is bound to inquire how walls necessary for the protection of the property against encroachment of the sea are maintained: there may be a covenant running with the land which would require him to contribute to the maintenance of sea walls along the boundaries of the levels in which the property is situated.

Raising banks

Whilst it follows from *Hudson* v. *Tabor, supra,* that a frontager on the coast may if he wishes erect works or raise banks to protect his property from the inroads of the sea, a riparian owner, whether on the banks of a tidal or non-tidal river, is not quite in the same position in times of flood. A riparian owner has the right to raise the river banks from time to time as it becomes necessary so as to confine the flood-water within the banks and prevent it from overflowing his land, provided he can do so without injury to others: *Ridge* v. *Midland Railway* (1888) 53 J.P. 55. This point was also brought out in *Birkett* v. *Morris* (1866) 30 J.P. 532, where the House of Lords decided that a riparian owner on a non-tidal river was entitled to build a bulwark *ripae mundi-endae causa* to protect his property from the invasion of the water, but was not at liberty to conduct his operation so as to cause actual injury to property on the other side of the river. In the earlier case of *Menzies* v. *Breadlane* (1828) 3 Bli. N.S. 414, a proprietor on the banks of a river was held to have no right to build a mound which, if completed, would in times of ordinary flood, throw the river water on the grounds of a proprietor on the opposite bank so as to overflow and injure them. There are, however, certain exceptions to this rule:

(a)   In the event of an extraordinary flood an owner may fence off his land to protect it and turn the flood away without regard to the consequences: *Nield* v. *London & N.W. Railway* (1874) 44 L.J. Ex. 15.

(b)   Where a riparian owner erects a flood embankment on his land half a mile from the river diagonally to its banks, he is not liable if the water flows in front of the embankment and on to his neighbour's land: *Gerrard* v. *Crowe* [1921] 1 A.C. 395.

(c)   A riparian owner may erect a mound to prevent the old course of the river from being gradually altered where part of the mound is erected on old foundations and it is the local custom of proprietors to so embank: *Farquharson* v. *Farquharson* (1741) Mor. 12, 787.

ARTIFICIAL WATER COURSES

Waterways of man-made construction, as opposed to natural water courses, have their own brand of law and do not necessarily attract riparian rights, as is indicated below.

Artificial watercourses are of common occurrence and in the course of but a short walk one seldom fails to encounter several specimens in the shape of sewers, canals and water mains. However, these are features of statutory origin and truer examples are to be found in mill streams into which water is diverted from a natural river to operate a mill, or in goits or cuts which discharge the drainage water from a mine or underground working to a nearby stream or pond.

The law regarding watercourses which are not of natural origin, but of artificial construction, is different from the law relating to rivers and streams as such, and at one time it was considered (*per* Lord Denman in *Magor* v. *Chadwick* (1840) 11 A. & E. 568) that the law of watercourses was the same whether natural or artificial. But this proposition was corrected when Sir Montagu Smith, delivering judgment in the case of *Rameshur Pershad Singh* v. *Koonj Behari Pattuck* (1878) 4 A.C. 121, remarked that "the right to water flowing in a natural channel and the right to water flowing through an artificial watercourse do not rest on the same principles. In the former case each successive riparian owner is entitled to the unimpeded flow of water in its natural course and to its reasonable enjoyment as it passes through his land as a natural incident to his ownership. In the latter case any right to the flow of water must rest on some grant or arrangement, from or with the owners of the lands from which the water is artificially brought or on some other legal 'origin.'"

Where an artificial channel is dug by a person on his own land and the water flowing down the channel rises on his land, no questions will normally arise about the rights and liabilities of other parties, but different considerations occur if the channel runs through the property of another person. The right to discharge water by means of an artificial watercourse across another's land does not exist as a natural right of property, but may be established as an easement by grant or long-continued enjoyment or under statute; the measure and extent of the right so acquired depending upon the terms of the deed of grant, the type of user or the provisions of the statute, as the case may be, in each case: *Sharp* v. *Waterhouse* (1857) 27 L.J.Q.B. 70; *Crossley* v. *Lightowler* (1867) 16 L.T. 438.

The right to an artificial channel as against the person creating it depends upon the character of the watercourse, whether it is of a permanent or temporary nature, upon the circumstances under which it was created, and the mode in which it has in fact been used and enjoyed: *Baily* v. *Clark & Morland* (1902) 86 L.T. 309.

Permanent Water courses and Riparian Rights

If the circumstances are such that it may be concluded that a watercourse is a permanent one, then prescriptive rights can be acquired and the riparian owners are in a position to exercise riparian rights in the water.

A watercourse, though artificial, may have been originally made under such circumstances and have been so used as to give all the rights that the riparian owners would have had if it had been a natural stream: *Sutcliffe* v. *Booth* (1863) 27 J.P. 613. In *Roberts* v. *Richards* (1881) 44 L.T. 271, a water-course which was partly natural and partly artificial, but so that nobody could tell when the artificial part was made, was deemed to be a natural watercourse, or if in part artificial to have been made so as to give all the rights of a riparian owner to the defendant and his predecessors in title. But where the origin of an artificial channel is unknown it may be possible to infer from the uses of the water and from other circumstances that the channel was originally constructed upon the condition that all the riparian owners should have the same rights as they would have had if the stream had been a natural one: *Baily* v. *Clark, supra.* The question of permanency also cropped up in *Gaved* v. *Martyn* (1865) 13 L.T. 74, which decided that a right to the flow of water along an artificial cut across another person's property cannot be acquired under the Prescription Act, 1832, unless the circumstances under which the cut was made show that it was intended to be of a permanent character.

The rights of riparian proprietors on the banks of an artificial stream were elaborated in *Wood* v. *Waud* (1849) 3 Ex. 748, in which the Court of Exchequer held that no action lay for an injury by the diversion of an artificial channel where it was obvious that the enjoyment of it depended on temporary circumstances and was not of a permanent character, and where the interruption was by a person who stood in the nature of a grantor. The court went on to emphasize that the enjoyment for 20 years of a stream diverted or penned up by permanent embankments clearly stood on a different footing from the enjoyment of a flow of water originating in the mode of occupation or alteration of a person's property and presumably of a temporary nature and liable to variation.

There are two further cases which throw some light on the status of riparian owners adjoining artificial streams. Where water flows through an artificial channel past the land of several owners to serve the purposes of an owner lower down, the proper grant to presume, in the absence of evidence as to the conditions upon which the channel was originally made, would be the grant of an easement or right to the running of water, and *prima facie* every landowner on the banks of the channel would be entitled to the moiety of the bed of the channel adjoining his land: *Whitmores v. Stanford* (1909) 99 L.T. 924. In *Nuthall* v. *Bracewell* (1866) 31 J.P. 8, where a natural stream was diverted down a goit in a lawful manner, the riparian owners in respect of the natural stream were held not to have lost their natural rights as a consequence of the water being diverted and flowing in the artificial channel.

Temporary Watercourses

If a watercourse is of a temporary character only, constructed for a temporary purpose, the owners on the banks cannot acquire any rights so as to preclude the watercourse being diverted or altered or the flow of water therein being stopped up.

In *Arkwright* v. *Gell* (1839) 5 M. & W. 203, the court decided that a stream draining a mine to a watercourse was an artificial one of a temporary character having its continuance only whilst the convenience of the mine owners required it and made with the sole object of getting rid of a nuisance to the mine. Consequently, owners of certain cotton mills situate on the banks of the stream which drained the mine had no right to compel the mine owners to continue the discharge. So also in *Burrows* v. *Lang* (1901) 84 L.T. 623, an ancient watercourse diverted from a natural stream and constructed and maintained solely for the purposes of a mill was held to be constructed for a temporary purpose and a purchaser of the mill acquired no right either by implied grant or under statute to the use of the water in the watercourse.

Following *Wood* v. *Waud, supra,* it was established in *Greatrex* v. *Hayward* (1853) 8 Ex. 291, that the flow of water for twenty years from a drain made for the purposes of agricultural improvements did not give a neighbour through whose land it flowed a right to the continuance of the flow, so as to preclude the proprietor of the land drained from altering his drains and so cutting off the supply. In accordance with these two cases, it was decided in *Bartlett* v. *Tottenham* (1932) 45 L.T. 686, that no prescriptive right could be acquired to receive water overflowing from a tank along an artificial stream which had been con-

structed for a temporary purpose only: *see* also *Hanna* v. *Pollock*
[1900] 2 I.R. 664. In any case, a person who makes an artificial cut
and so brings water to a stream which did not go there before, can
prima facie cut it off if he chooses: *Brymbo Water Co.* v. *Lesters Lime
Co.* (1894) 8 R. 329.

Pollution of Artificial Watercourses

In cases where it can be concluded that an artificial channel was
made in such circumstances as to give the owners on the banks riparian
rights (*vide Sutcliffe* v. *Booth* and other cases, *supra*), it appears that
the riparian owners have the same remedies to prevent pollution as have
the owners on the banks of a natural river.

With regard to temporary watercourses constructed for a temporary
purpose, the decisions are somewhat conflicting. In *Whaley* v. *Laing*
(1857) 26 L.J. Ex. 327, the court held that a mere licensee using water
from a canal could maintain an action against anyone passing foul water
to his premises, but *Ormerod* v. *Todmorden Mill Co.* (1883) 47 J.P. 532
(following *Stockport Waterworks Co.* v. *Potter* (1861) 26 J.P. 56)
decided that a water company, not being riparian owners, taking water
from a natural stream by means of conduits had no natural rights which
entitled them to sue a higher riparian owner on the stream for polluting
the stream whereby the water flowing through the conduits was also
fouled. Finally, in *Magor* v. *Chadwick* (1840) 9 L.J.Q.B. 159, it was
said that an owner on the banks of an artificial channel might bring an
action to prevent the channel being polluted on the grounds that no
one is entitled to discharge foul water on to another's premises in the
absence of a legal right to do so: *see* also *Wood* v. *Waud*, and *Ballard* v.
Tomlinson (1885) 49 J.P. 692. As matters stand, it is probably the
wiser course not to attempt to extract any guiding principles from these
cases for the present.

FERRIES

Rivers are interrupted all too frequently and physically both by transport devices, such as bridges, fords and ferries, and by service installations, i.e., water mains, sewers, drains, gas and other pipes, wires, cables and so forth. Each and all these objects have their own individual law and ferries have been chosen as an example.

The word "ferry" can be used, quite accurately, to connote different though related things, Fortunately, its use in different senses (unlike the use of some legal and semi-legal expressions) can hardly cause confusion. It can refer to an object, which may be anything from a rowing-boat operated by one man carrying foot-passengers across a small river up to a large steamer capable of conveying vehicles, passengers, and goods across miles of sea. In law the word indicates the right to operate such a boat, and also a special sort of highway, for all the Queen's subjects paying toll (*North and South Shields Ferry Co.* v. *Barker* (1848) 2 Ex. 136), which may be described as the continuation of a public highway across a river or other water for the purpose of taking public traffic from the termination of the highway on the one side to its recommencement on the other side: *Letton* v. *Gooden* (1866) 30 J.P. 677. A public ferry, however, is a highway of a special description and its termini must be places where the public have rights, such as towns or vills, or highways leading to towns or vills. In the one case the grantee of the ferry has the exclusive right of carrying passengers, animals or goods by boat over a river or an arm of the sea from town to town; in the other, he has a similar right of carrying from one point to the other all who are going to use the highway to the nearest town of vill to which the highway leads on the other side: *Huzzey* v. *Field* (1835) 5 Tyr 855.

The owner of a ferry must have a right to use the land on both sides of the water for the purpose of embarking and disembarking his passengers, but he need not have any property in the soil on either side (*Peter* v. *Kendal* (1827) 6 B. & C. 703) and the owner may be said to have a right to make a special use of the highway, although he does not have the occupation of the highway: *R.* v. *Nicholson* (1810) 12 East 330. It is not essential that the ferry owner should own the land on either side if he has the right of using that land for the purpose of the ferry: *R.* v. *Great Northern Rly.* (1849) 14 Q.B. 25. A ferry is not a servitude imposed upon a district or large area of land, and is wholly unconnected with the ownership or occupation of land: *Newton* v. *Cubitt* (1862) 6 L.T. 86.

A ferry may exist across a tidal creek although at a low tide it is possible to cross the creek on foot by means of a public causeway (*Layzell* v. *Thompson* (1926) 91 J.P. 89), and a floating bridge consisting of a vessel propelled by steam from one side of a river to the other and kept on its course by chains laid down across the bed of the stream is in substance a ferry and not a bridge: *Ward* v. *Gray* (1865) 29 J.P. 470. A ferry, in the sense of a right, is an incorporeal hereditament and must be transferred by deed, and a lease of it must also be by deed (*Mayfield* v. *Robinson* (1845) 7 Q.B. 486), and being a franchise and therefore a hereditament, a ferry is "lands" within the definition of s.3 of the Lands Clauses Consolidation Act, 1845: *R.* v. *Cambrian Rly.* (1871) L.R. 6 Q.B. 422.

A distinction for the purpose of classification may be made between (1) ancient franchise ferries, and (2) statutory ferries.

FRANCHISE FERRIES

A franchise ferry is an ancient ferry having its origin in Royal grant or licence or in prescription, which presumes a Royal grant. There are very few cases known of an actual grant of ferry rights made by the Crown (*see Pim* v. *Curell* (1840) 6 M. & W. 234) and a claim to a ferry is usually established by prescription at common law or by presumption of a lost grant. The jury may presume that a ferry has a legal origin from a user of 35 years, and a variation in the amount of ferriage will not avoid the franchise, though the owner may be liable for extortion: *Trotter* v. *Harris* (1828) 2 Y. & J. 285. The grant of a ferry by the Crown is a valid grant, although made since Magna Carta, and a charter from the Crown granting "all our ferriages and passages" over certain rivers conveys only ferries existing at the date of the grant and does not confer on the grantee the right to create new ferries over those rivers: *Londonderry Bridge Commissioners* v. *M'Keever* (1890) 27 L.R. Ir. 464.

A franchise ferry may be of two kinds; the more common type being known as a point to point ferry, being an exclusive right only to ferry persons coming along a public way to a landing place and desiring to cross to a landing place on the opposite bank and continue their journey

along another public way: *Hammerton* v. *Dysart (Earl)* (1916) 80 J.P.
97. The other type of ferry is a vill to vill ferry, which is an exclusive
right of ferriage from one vill to another throughout the area of the
vills: *General Estates Co.* v. *Beaver* (1914) 79 J.P. 41. In the case of a
point to point ferry the termini cannot be varied to any substantial
extent; in a vill to vill ferry the termini may be varied within the limits
of the vills: *Hammerton* v. *Dysart (Earl), supra.*

The right to take tolls from customers is usually part of the franchise
provided it is founded on adequate consideration as between the public
and the grantee, that is to keep up a boat for the passage over a stream
not otherwise fordable; and the toll must be reasonable in amount, for
where the tolls granted are outrageous, the franchise is illegal and void:
Mayor of Nottingham v. *Lambert* (1738) Willes 111. A franchise ferry
carries with it the right to take reasonable toll from the passengers
(*Hale, De Jure Maris,* cited in *A.-G.* v. *Simpson* (1901) 85 L.T. 325, and
Simpson v. *A.-G* (1904) 60 J.P. 85, unless the ferry is toll-free by local
custom, and within the limits of an ancient ferry no one is permitted to
convey passengers across except the owner of the ferry. No one may
disturb the ferry, which carries with it an exclusive right or monopoly,
and in consideration of the monopoly the ferry owner is bound to have
his ferry always ready: *Payne* v. *Partridge* (1691) 1 Salk 12.

The owner of a franchise ferry has onerous duties to observe. He is
under the obligation of always providing proper boats with competent
boatmen and all other things necessary for the maintenance of the ferry
in an efficient state and condition for the use of the public, and this he
is bound to do under pain of indictment: *Letton* v. *Gooden, supra.* He
must be prepared at all reasonable times to ferry those who wish to be
ferried and cannot discriminate between passengers. He is, and must
remain, a servant of the public: *Hammerton* v. *Dysart (Earl), supra.*

If the owner of a franchise ferry fails to maintain it and keep it in
repair, he is liable to indictment for misdemeanour for neglect, and the
grant of franchise may be revoked by the Crown on *scire facias* or *quo
warranto* and may be vested in another person, if he does not perform
his duty: *Peter* v. *Kendal, supra.* The owner cannot suppress the ferry
and erect a bridge across the river in lieu without licence and *ad quod
damnum.* An action will, however, not lie against the ferryman for not
keeping a boat for the purpose of the ferry unless some special damage
ensues: *Payne* v. *Partridge, supra.* In *A.-G and Another* v. *Hudson,
Hudson and Palmer* (1899) A.C., unreported, it was decided that
Medmenham Ferry on the Thames and an ancient franchise ferry
for horses, carriages, and foot-passengers, and that the owner thereof
was liable to maintain such ferry and that a highway existed on both
sides of the ferry. In *Pelly* v. *Woodbridge U.D.C.* (1950) 114 J.P.N.
666, the court refused to grant an interlocutory mandatory injunction
to restrain the defendant council from discontinuing a public ferry.

Subsequently, in *A.-G., ex rel. Allen* v. *Colchester Corporation* [1955] 2 All E.R. 124, it was decided that where a local authority, which owned the franchise of a public ferry, determined its operation on the grounds that the ferry was not extensively used and that the toll charged was insuffieient to pay the ferryman's wages, a mandatory injunction must be refused and a bare declaration would be of no service to the relator or other inhabitants, because it would be inequitable to compel the authority to work the ferry on pain of imprisonment or sequestration.

The ferryman is liable if an injury is caused to passengers, animals, or goods because the ferry has not been kept in a proper state of repair: *Dalyell* v. *Tyrer* (1858) 5 Jur. N.S. 335; *Willoughby* v. *Horridge* (1852) 16 J.P. 761; *Coote* v. *Lear* (1886) 2 T.L.R. 806. The owner of a ferry for carriages is bound to convey carriages and their contents: *Walker* v. *Jackson* (1843) 10 M. & W. 161. If a ferryman surcharges his boat, then in case of necessity any passenger may cast the things out of the boat for the safety of the lives of the passengers, and the owners have their remedy against the ferryman. But if there is no surcharging and danger accrues only by the act of God and not through the default of the ferrymen, every one should bear his own loss: *Mouse's Case* (1608) 2 Bulst. 280. A ferry boat which continues to operate in time of fog takes upon herself the responsibility incident to such a course, and cannot set up public convenience against the probability of loss to life and property, and will be liable for damage done to other vessels with which she may come into collision, provided those vessels take the precautions required by law to warn her of their position: *The Lancashire* (1874) 2 Asp. 202.

Since a ferry is in the nature of a monopoly the owner is entitled to protect his exclusive right by action in the courts. The owner of a ferry has a cause of action in nuisance against any one who sets up a ferry either in the line of the ancient ferry or in another line of ferry so near as to make it an alternative way of carrying between substantially the same points: *Hammerton* v. *Dysart (Earl), supra,* in which a ferry was set up across the Thames within a quarter of a mile from one of the termini of an ancient ferry. The House of Lords held that the owner of the old ferry had no cause of action since the new ferry carried a new and different kind of traffic, the bulk of which had been created by the erection of the rival ferry, and which, but for such ferry, would not have existed at all, that is would not have increased either the profits or burdens of the owner of the franchise. In *Newton* v. *Cubitt, supra,* it was said that "if the public convenience require a new passage at such a distance from the old ferry as makes it to be a real convenience to the public, the proximity seems to us not actionable". Where a ferry connects two points, a person who uses the ferry from one point of the old ferry to a different point on the other side does not disturb the old ferry, provided that it is not done fraudulently and as a pretence for avoiding the regular ferry: *Tripp* v. *Frank* (1792) 4 T.R. 666. A plaintiff can maintain an action for disturbance by providing that he was in possession of the ferry at the time the cause of action accrued; it is not necessary that he should show receipts of tolls from passengerrs: *Peter* v. *Kendal, supra.*

A ferry owner cannot maintain an action for loss of traffic caused by a new highway by bridge or ferry made to provide for a new traffic, since the owner of a ferry has not a grant of an exclusive right of carrying passengers and goods across the stream by any means whatever, but only a grant of an exclusive right to carry them across by means of a ferry: *Hopkins* v. *Great Northern Railway* (1877) 42 J.P. 229, overruling *R.* v. *Cambrian Railway, supra.* In *Dibden* v. *Skirrow* (1908) 71 J.P.555, where a bridge was constructed by private enterprise connecting the same highways as the ferry, so that the ferry owner lost all the income he used to receive by tolls, it was held that the bridge was not a disturbance of the ferry, and the ferry owner had no remedy.

STATUTORY FERRIES

The characteristics and limits of a statutory ferry are governed by the Act of Parliament establishing the ferry, and modern ferries owe their existence to their creation by statute; whether a local Act, conferring a right to maintain a ferry service, contains a grant of an exclusive ferry is a matter of its construction: *Bournemouth-Swanage Motor Road and Ferry Co.* v. *Harvey and Sons* (1930) 93 J.P. 9, which case also decided that a landing stage constructed by the plaintiffs under their private Act was the private property of the ferry company and that they were entitled to prevent any one from using it except in connexion with their ferry and on payment of the appropriate tolls. No action will lie for the disturbance of a ferry created by Act of Parliament if, according to the true construction of the Act, no obligation exists on the part of the ferry owner towards the public: *Letton* v. *Gooden, supra.*

GENERAL ACTS AFFECTING FERRIES

The Ferries (Acquisition by Local Authorities) Act, 1919, enables a local authority i.e. a county council or district council, to purchase or accept the transfer of an existing ferry which is within the area of the local authority or which serves the inhabitants of that area. "Existing ferry" means any ferry legally established by Act of Parliament or otherwise at the date of purchase or transfer, and includes all boats and other vessels, landing stages, approaches, plant and other property used in connexion with the ferry. Subject to the provisions of any Act of Parliament under which the ferry was established, and to the rights of any other persons, the local authority may work, maintain and improve the ferry and charge such tolls as were legally chargeable in respect of the ferry before the sale or transfer, or such other tolls as the local authority may determine with the approval of the Secretary of State for the Environment. The local authority may, with the Secretary of State's approval, free the ferry from tolls and shall have the same rights and liabilities which the owner of the ferry possessed or to which he was subject. Local authorities may join together for the purchase or acceptance, working, maintenance, or improvement of a ferry under the Act, or may contribute towards the expenses thereof. The local authority must make regulations with regard to the working of a ferry acquired under the Act for the protection from injury of passengers and the general public, and such regulations have to be confirmed by the Secretary of State.

Where the Secretary of State for the Environment has approved proposals under the National Parks and Access to the Countryside Act, 1949, relating to a long-distance route, which include proposals for the provision and operation of a ferry needed for completing the route, the highway authority for either or both of the highways to be connected by the ferry shall be empowered to provide and operate the ferry and to carry out such work and do all things as appear to them expedient for the purpose of operating the ferry. The highway authority may also, with the approval of the Secretary of State make arrangements for any person to provide and operate the ferry and make such contributions as may be agreed with that person. These powers are not to be construed as conferring an exclusive right to operate a ferry and persons having such an exclusive right are protected (*see* further s.53 of the National Parks, etc., Act, 1949). Road ferries may be provided, maintained and improved by a local highway authority (Highways Act, 1959, ss.26, 107).

EXTINGUISHMENT OF FERRIES

Neglect of duty by the ferry owner does not *ipso facto* destroy the franchise of a ferry, but the Crown may repeal the grant or the owner may relinquish his interest in the ferry by surrender of the lease: *Peter* v. *Kendal, supra*. A ferry may be extinguished by statute, *e.g.*, where an Act of Parliament authorizes the substitution of a bridge or modern ferry for an ancient ferry: *Cory* v. *Yarmouth and Norwich Railway* (1844) 3 Hare 593.

THE RULE OF THE RIVER

A navigable river which carries traffic requires rules to control the navigation, and to regulate the powers and liabilities of river users and those who govern the navigation.

Within the last few years the public have taken more and more to frequenting inland waterways, in vessels of various sorts and sizes, for pleasure and recreation — in much the same way as they earlier invaded the highways in cars and on motor-cycles and bicycles. Whilst this is by no means a new national pastime (since these islands have always produced enthusiasts for boat and sail), the popularity of the motor cruiser and the outboard motor have greatly added to the river population in summer. New techniques in small boat construction, including the provision of glass-fibre and plastic-type hulls, have also played their part. Anyone who doubts the truth of this should visit the National Boat Show.

River users can be separated into several classes. Those who can afford to do so may acquire a motor cruiser, whilst the energetic and the young often join a sailing or boating club. Others for a holiday will hire a cruiser by the week and tour the inland navigation systems or what remains of them. Then there are those who take out a small boat for the day or hour, or prefer to view the passing scenery from the deck or saloon of a pleasure steamer. These comprise the pleasure traffic of the river, and should be distinguished from the merchandise traffic consisting of barges, lighters, and tugs, and also from "official" craft such as fire-floats, police tenders, and craft employed by navigation and harbour authorities, *e.g.*, patrol launches, dredgers, and wreck-raising vessels. Additionally, there may be house-boats and converted craft used both for week-end and permanent residence.

The purpose here is to discuss the law as it affects the use of a navigable river, and there are three aspects of this. First, what is the position of a person navigating a vessel on the river? Secondly, what are the liabilities of owners of accommodation, *e.g.*, wharves, moorings, etc., on the river? And thirdly, what are the responsibilities of the navigation authority for maintaining the river?

Rights and Duties of Navigators

Navigable rivers are public highways navigable by the public in reasonable manner and for a reasonable purpose *(Original Hartlepool Colleries Co.* v. *Gibb* (1877) 41 J.P. 660) and a person navigating a boat on a tidal navigable river has a right of passage over the whole of the navigable channel: *A.-G* v. *Terry* (1874) 38 J.P. 340. But the right of public navigation on non-tidal waters is limited to the extent that the right is made available by the grant, dedication, user, or statute conferring the right, and there is no right of navigation over a river if the use made of the river is permissive and not of right: *Bourke* v. *Davis* (1889) 62 L.T. 34. The right of navigation in rivers takes precedence over the right of fishers: *Gann* v. *Free Fishers of Whitstable* (1865) 12 L.T. 150.

A navigator on an inland river has no right of public fishing: *Smith* v. *Andrews* [1891] 2 Ch. 678, unless the waters are tidal. Nor has he any property in the bed and soil of the river: *Orr Ewing* v. *Colquhoun* [1877] 2 A.C. 839; and he cannot land or embark on the bank except at places properly appointed for such purposes, such as a public landing stage or draw-dock: *Behrens* v. *Richards* (1905) 69 J.P. 381.

A person in control of a vessel on an inland navigation is under a duty to take reasonable care and to use reasonable skill to prevent the vessel from doing injury, and negligence on his part may be represented by his failure to observe the rules of good seamanship (which form part of the general maritime law) or by a breach of the international or local regulations for preventing collisions.

The international regulations are set out in the Collision Regulations *(vide* S.I.1977 No. 982) made pursuant to s.418 of the Merchant Shipping Act, 1894, and must be observed by vessels upon the high seas and in all waters connected therewith navigable by seagoing vessels, but do not apply where local rules have been made for the navigation of a harbour, river, lake or inland water. Most navigable rivers, etc., in England possess their own rules, which are largely based on the Collision Regulations and suitably adapted to meet local circumstances. The regulations *(inter alia)* prescribe the lights to be shown by vessels at night, sound signals to be emitted by boats in adverse weather and under certain conditions, and rules for steering and sailing.

Having disposed, rather cursorily, of the rules of navigation, it is interesting to note some of the more usual hazards likely to confront the river user. Two great temptations with which the inexperienced navigator may be faced are improper navigation and speeding.

Persons navigating a river improperly, either by too much speed or by negligent conduct, are as much liable if death ensues as are those who cause it on a proper highway on land, either by furious driving or by negligent conduct: *R.* v. *Taylor* (1840) 9 C. & P. 672. A river being a public highway must as a rule be be kept open and free from damage for all vessels navigating thereon: *The Vianna* (1858) Sw. 405. There are usually no fixed speed limits on a river, but excessive speed is discouraged because the resultant wake from a quickly driven craft may assist erosion of banks, swamp or overturn smaller vessels, injure riparian property, and generally lead to a lot of bad feeling on the part of other river users. To quote an example as to the way in which the legislature has dealt with river navigation, s.97 of the Thames Conservancy Act, 1932, provides that "every vessel navigating the Thames shall be navigated with care and caution and at such a speed and in such a manner as not to endanger the lives of or cause injury to persons or endanger the safety of or cause damage to other vessels or any moorings or to the banks of the Thames or other property" and "the person in charge of any vessel who is navigating such vessel contravenes or fails to observe the provisions of this section shall for every such offence be liable to a penalty not exceeding £20." This enables each case of careless or negligent navigation, including a case of exessive speed, to be dealt with on its merits.

On the subject of speed generally, it was said in *The Europa* (1850) 14 Jur. 627 that "no rate of sailing by steamers or other vessels can be said absolutely to be dangerous, but whether any given rate is dangerous or not must depend upon the circumstances of each individual case, as the state of the weather, locality and other similar facts. When a ship is sailing at a rapid rate, her master and crew are bound to exercise greater caution." It is noteworthy that as early as 1838 the Corporation of London made a byelaw imposing a penalty on all persons navigating steam vessels on the Thames at a greater rate than five miles per hour.

Liabilities of Owners of River Accommodations

The owner of an obstruction (such as a pile) placed negligently in or on a navigable river is responsible for any injury caused thereby to a person navigating the river (*Brownlow* v. *Metropolitan Board of Works* (1864) 6 L.T. 187), and the owner of an erection on the banks of a navigable river is liable for damage caused by want of repair of the erection, unless he gives notice of the danger: *White* v. *Phillips* (1863) 9 L.T. 388. A port authority who provide moorings in a river for vessels are not under an absolute duty to keep the mooring buoys fit for the purposes for which they are used, but only under a duty to take all reasonable steps to see that the buoys are so fit: *Williams & Sons, Ltd.,* v. *Port of London Authority* (1933) 39 Com. Cas. 77.

A wharfinger who invites vessels to berth alongside his property is liable for any injury to the vessel caused by the uneven condition of the river bottom, unless he has taken reasonable care to ascertain that the berth was safe to use (*The Monarch* (1889) 60 L.T. 654), or has warned the owner of the vessel that he has not done so: *The Grit* (1924) 132 L.T. 638. It makes no difference if the wharfinger is not the owner of the river bed or makes no charge for landing and storage.

Responsibilities of Navigation Authority for Maintaining the River

The control and upkeep of most inland navigable waterways is in the hands of some body usually established by Act of Parliament, whether it be trustees, commissioners, a conservancy board, navigation company, or a port or harbour undertaking, and occasionally a water authority.

At common law a navigation authority who are empowered by statute to render a river navigable and to take tolls to meet the expenses thereof are under no obligation to cut weeds or dredge silt, unless it is necessary to do so for the improvement of navigation; *Cracknell* v. *Thetford Corporation* (1869) L.R. 4 C.P. 629; *Hodgson* v. *York Corporation* (1873) 37 J.P. 725. Nor is a landowner, who is authorized by Act of Parliament to improve the navigation of a river running through his land, liable to maintain or repair the locks: *A.-G* v. *Simpson* (1904) 69 J.P. 85. But the governing factor in each case is the effect of the navigation statute which may, *e.g.*, provide for the payment of compensation to persons injuriously affected by the exercise of the navigation authority's statutory powers: *R*. v. *Delamere* (1965) 13 W.R. 757.

The general result of the above cases is to indicate that a navigation authority are not under a strict obligation to keep the navigation in proper repair; but an authority who open the navigation to the public upon payment of tolls are under a duty at common law, not perhaps to repair the navigation or absolutely free it from obstructions, but to take reasonable care, so long as they keep it open for the public use of all who choose to navigate it, that the public may navigate without danger to their lives or property. "The authority are responsible for a breach of this duty upon a similar principle to that which makes a shopkeeper, who invites the public to his shop, liable for neglect on leaving a trapdoor open without any protection, by which the customers suffer injury"; *Parnaby* v. *Lancaster Canal Co.* (1839) 11 A. & E. 223. This principle applies whether the tolls taken are for the profit of the authority or are devoted to the maintenance of the navigation works: *Mersey Docks* v. *Gibbs* (1864) 14 L.T. 677. But it appears that where tolls are not taken no liability exists to carry out repairs or to remove obstructions: *Forbes* v. *Lee Conservancy Board* (1879) 4 Ex. D. 116.

Following *Parnaby* v. *Lancaster Canal Co.* and *Mersey Docks* v.

Gibbs, came *Winch* v. *Thames Conservators* (1872) 36 J.P. 646. Here the plaintiffs claimed damages for the loss of some horses drowned whilst towing a barge, due to the fact that part of the Thames towpath was out of repair. The defendants did not own the towpath but had the use thereof, and took an aggregate toll for the use of the whole of the navigation. *Held*: that so long as the defendants kept open the towpath and took tolls for its use they were under an obligation to those whom they invited to use the towpath to take reasonable care to see that it was in such a state as not to expose those using it to undue danger, and the defendants were accordingly liable. But the Court (*per* Bramwell, B.) left a loophole for the conservancy authority by saying "the defendants can in future if they think fit announce to those who pay the tolls that they must take the towpaths as they find them, and if this is done there could be no liability for a defective state of repair, even though wilful."

The doctrine of the duty of "reasonable care" has been qualified in two respects by two later cases. In *Gridley* v. *Thames Conservators* (1886) 3 T.L.R. 108, the plaintiff sought to recover damages for injuries sustained by his barge whilst moored at a wharf; when the tide ebbed the barge grounded and was strained through the unsafe condition of the shore bottom. The Court decided, first, that the barge had stopped to unload and that the navigation could not be said to be going on. Even if it were, the Conservators' duty was only to take care that the part of the river ordinarily used for navigation was safe. This part was not so used so their duty did not extend to that place. Secondly, the court went on to say, "but, even if there was such a duty imposed on them, there was no evidence that they knew or ought to have known the state of the bottom, and so there was no negligence on their part."

This second qualification was affirmed by the Court of Appeal in *Queens of the River S.S. Co.* v. *Eastern Gibb & Co. and Thames Conservators* (1907) 96 L.T. 901 (see, also, *Stevens* v. *Thames Conservators* [1958] 1 Lloyds Rep. 401), where the plaintiffs' paddle steamer struck on a submerged pile in the bed of the Thames while navigating the centre arch of Kew Bridge. The Court concluded that the defendants had no knowledge of the danger arising from the pile or the fact that it was there, and that there was no neglect of examination or supervision by the defendants' servants which led to their being negligently ignorant of the danger that was there.

UNDERGROUND WATER

Water in underground strata, which possesses different principles to water flowing on the surface has attracted its own branch of case law, and, more latterly, statute law.

Surface water, whether flowing in rivers and streams, or static in lakes and ponds, is everywhere to be seen in abundance in this country. But water beneath the ground, which is just as plentiful, is apparent only when it emerges to the surface in the form of springs or is drawn up out of a well or is pumped up through a borehole although the presence of aquifers and the quantity and quality of water therein is under investigation. A convenient start can be made by considering some of the law relating to springs, wells and boreholes.

Springs, Wells and Boreholes

A spring of water, both in law and ordinary language, is a natural source of water of a definite and well-marked extent: *Taylor* v. *St. Helen's Corporation* (1877) 37 L.T. 253. Another definition of a spring is given in *Brain* v. *Marfell* (1879) 41 L.T. 457, *viz.* " a spring is not an artificial space, but a natural chasm in which water has collected and from which it is lost by percolation or rises in a defined channel." A right to take water from a well by reason of the occupation of a dwelling-house, and for the more convenient occupation thereof, is an interest in land (*Tyler* v. *Bennett* (1836) 5 Ad. & El. 377), and water as it issues from a spring or well is not to be considered as the produce of the soil so as to make the right to take it *in alieno solo* for domestic purposes a *profit a prendre*; such right is an easement only and may be claimed by custom; *Race* v. *Ward* (1855) 19 J.P. 563. After twenty years uninterrupted enjoyment of a spring of water an absolute right to it is gained by the owner of the land in which it issues above ground and an adjoining owner cannot lawfully cut a drain whereby the supply of water to the spring is diminished: *Balston* v. *Bensted* (1808) 1 Camp 463.

44

A landowner is entitled to sink a shaft on his land for the abstraction of water percolating underground through his land (*Bradford Corporation* v. *Pickles* (1895) 60 J.P. 3), but it is an offence to abstract water contained in underground strata except pursuant to a licence issued by the water authority under Part IV of the Water Resources Act, 1963. It is also illegal to construct a well, borehole or other work whereby water may be abstracted from underground strata, or to extend a well, borehole or other work, or to instal or modify machinery or apparatus whereby additional quantities of water may be abstracted from such strata by means of a well, borehole or other work, unless the water abstracted or additional quantities of water is authorised by a licence and the construction or extension, etc. fulfills the requirements of such licence as to the means whereby water is authorised to be abstracted. A licence is not required in certain circumstances, such as (1) if the construction is for the purpose of abstracting water solely and to the extent necessary for a supply of domestic household water; (2) for experimental boring for the purpose of ascertaining the presence of underground water or the quality or quantity of such water if the work is carried out with the consent of the water authority.

Types of Underground Water

Lord Chelmsford in *Chasemore* v. *Richards* (1859) 23 J.P. 596, drew a distinction between " a known subterranean channel flowing in a certain and defined course" and "water percolating through underground strata, which has no certain course, no defined limits, but oozes through the soil in every direction in which the rain penetrates." Legally speaking, there is no great distinction between the rights relating to water flowing in a defined channel on the surface and rights of water flowing in known and defined underground channels, and it was stated in *M'Nab* v. *Robertson* [1897] A.C. 129, that "a subterranean flow of water may in some circumstances possess the very same characteristics as a body of water running on the surface."

The meaning of a "known and defined channel" has been considered on a number of occasions by the courts, starting with two Irish cases.

A "defined" channel means a contracted and bounded channel, although the course of the stream may be undefined by human knowledge; "known" means the knowledge by reasonable inference from existing and observed facts in the natural or pre-existing condition of the surface of the ground and is not synonymous with "visible," nor is it restricted to knowledge dervied from exposure of the channel by excavation: *Black* v. *Ballymena Commissioners* (1886) 17 L.R.Ir. 459. In order to apply the rule as to riparian rights to subterranean water, it must flow not only in a defined channel but in a known channel, giving to the word "known" a sense beyond what is conveyed by the word "defined": *Ewart* v. *Belfast Poor Law Commissioners* (1881) 9 L.R.Ir.

172, in which case underground water was only discovered by deep excavations made in the land under which the water flowed, and even then it was a matter of some doubt whether there was a defined channel.

These two Irish decisions have been considered in later English cases. In *Bradford Corporation* v. *Ferrand* (1902) 67 J.P. 21, it was held that if underground water flows in a defined channel into a well supplying a stream above ground, but the existence and course of the channel are not known and cannot be defined except by excavation, the lower riparian owners on the banks of the stream have no right of action for the abstraction of the underground water. *Bleachers' Association, Ltd.* v. *Chapel-en-le-Frith R.D.C.* (1933) 96 J.P. 515 applied the meaning of the words "defined" and "known" given in the Ballymena case and, in considering *Bradford Corporation* v. *Ferrand*, thought that the head-note thereto should be amended by reading into it the word "subsequent" before the word "excavation."

Now going back to the distinction made between the two types of underground water in *Chasemore* v. *Richards, supra*, it was also pointed out in that case that the principles which regulate the rights of land-owners in respect of water flowing in known and defined channels, whether upon or below the surface of the ground, do not apply to underground water which merely percolates through the strata in no defined channels, and, to quote but one example, underground water not flowing in a channel cannot be the subject of property or capable of being conveyed: *Ewart* v. *Belfast Poor Law Commissioners, supra*. The remainder of this is concerned with the law relating to underground percolating water which has no defined course.

Abstraction of Underground Water

Most of the law which has been built up in relation to underground water is concerned, not unnaturally, with the abstraction or interception of such water. It will be borne in mind that the cases referred to here below were decided long before any statutory restrictions became imposed on abstracting water from underground strata in the form that a prior licence is now necessary from the water authority. The keystone of the case law on abstraction is *Chasemore* v. *Richards*, already referred to, but before dealing with that case two earlier decisions should be mentioned.

Acton v. *Blundell* (1843) 13 L.J.Ex. 289, stated that the owner of land through which water flows in a subterranean course has no right or interest in it which enables him to maintain an action against a land-owner who, in conducting mining operations in his own land in the usual way, drains away the water from the land of the first-mentioned owner and leaves his well dry. In *Dickinson* v. *Grand Junction Canal Co.* (1852) 7 Ex. 282, where a land-owner by digging a well prevented underground water from reaching a river which it would otherwise have reached, it was held that an action would lie against the land-owner by a riparian owner for injury to his right, whether the underground water was part of an underground channel or percolated through the strata.

Acton v. *Blundell* was followed, but the *Dickenson* case was overruled, in *Chasemore* v. *Richards, supra*, where a mill owner who had for more than 20 years enjoyed the use of a stream, which was chiefly supplied by percolating and underground water, lost the use of the stream after an adjoining landowner had dug on his own land an extensive well for the purpose of supplying water to the inhabitants of the district, many of whom had no title as landowners to the use of the water. The House of Lords decided that the mill owner could not maintain an action for the interception of the underground percolating water.

There have been a number of decisions in the wake of *Chasemore* v. *Richards* which have defined more concisely the circumstances and limits within which percolating water can be abstracted or intercepted without giving rise to a right of action against the person whose works are responsible for the abstraction, by an owner whose supply of water is diminished as a result of the abstraction. Generally speaking, where underground percolating water is intercepted (*a*) before it has reached a well, or (*b*) when it has reached and is actually in a well, no action will lie, but if percolating water is abstracted (1) as it issues from the ground as a natural spring and before it flows in a defined channel from its source, or (2) where it has arrived in a defined channel on the surface, a right of action arises.

Taken individually, these cases form useful extensions to the decision in *Chasemore* v. *Richards*, but considering the cases collectively it is difficult to establish any general secondary rules which run either concurrently with or consecutively to *Chasemore* v. *Richards*. For instance, it cannot be concluded from these cases that percolating water, once it reaches the surface, will be subject to the same rules which govern water flowing on the surface, since percolating water does not necessarily flow in a defined surface channel, as to which *see M'Nab* v. *Robertson, supra*. In that case, it was held that where a person sinks a tank near some ponds and draws off from marshy ground percolating water which would have found its way eventually to one of the ponds, the water percolating through the ground towards the pond is not water in any stream leading to the pond. For other cases on casual surface water *see Rawstron* v. *Taylor* (1855) 11 Ex. 369; *Broadbent* v. *Ramsbotham* (1856) 11 Ex. 602; *Bartlett* v.*Tottenham* [1932] 1 Ch. 114.

The decisions following *Chasemore* v. *Richards* start with *Dudden* v. *Clutton Union* (1857) 1 H. & N. 627, concerning a natural stream of water arising from a spring which served the plaintiff's well. The defendants sank a well in the ground for their workhouse and caught the water as it arose from the earth. *Held*: that this was not taking underground percolating water, but water after it had arrived at the spring-head, and the plaintiff therefore succeeded. The principle is not affected by the fact that the source of the spring has been built round and formed into a well, resulting in an artificial channel for a short distance: *Mostyn* v. *Atherton* (1899) 81 L.T. 356.

In *Brain* v. *Marfell* (1879) 44 J.P. 56, the defendant sold the plaintiff a well and the right to convey water therefrom through the defendant's land without interruption. The court decided that the defendant had only conveyed the flow of water after it had risen in the well and that no action could lie for interception of percolating water before it reached the well. Where water which has actually percolated into and is in a well has been abstracted by operations in the adjoining land, no action will lie: *New River Co.* v. *Johnson* (1860) 24 J.P. 244.

Although a landowner will not in general be restrained from drawing off the subterranean waters in the adjoining land, he will be restrained if in so doing he abstracts the water flowing in a defined surface channel through the adjoining land: *Grand Junction Canal Co.* v. *Shugar* (1871) 35 J.P. 660. But contrast this with *English* v. *Metropolitan Water Board* (1907) 71 J.P. 313, where the defendant's pumping from a well led to the general lowering of the water in the neighbouring soil, causing the soil to become dry, and a portion of the water flowing down a nearby stream leaked out through the bed and side of the stream, and the supply of water to a lower riparian owner was sensibly diminished, though none of the water which leaked out reached the well. It was held that the riparian owner had no cause of action against the person pumping the well because the injury was caused by the withdrawal of support and not by abstraction from the stream.

A landowner is not entitled to compensation under statute for the abstraction of water from underground springs, which rose in his land and fed his ponds, by a sewer made under the authority of the statute, in neighbouring land, since compensation can only be claimed where the damage would have been a ground of action if arising from the act of a private individual, and, as the abstraction of underground water was not actionable, compensation could not be claimed: *R.* v. *Metropolitan Board of Works* (1863) 27 J.P. 342.

In *Bunting* v. *Hicks* (1894) 70 L.T. 455, pumping from the defendant's well reduced the general water level in the adjacent soil, with the result that some water flowing in a nearby stream leaked out through the bed and banks and thereby reduced the flow of water in the stream, to the detriment of a lower riparian owner. *Held*, following *English* v. *Metropolitan Water Board, supra,* and distinguishing *Grand Junction Canal Co.* v. *Shugar, supra,* that the riparian owner had no cause of action, as the defendant did not appropriate any of the stream water by his pumping, but only caused it to sink into the ground by withdrawing the support of underground water.

The last of the major decisions following *Chasemore* v. *Richards* is apparently *Bradford Corporation* v. *Pickles, supra.* Here the respondent sank a shaft on his land to a spring from which the water undertakers derived part of their supply, and he also drove a level through his land for draining the strata for working minerals. These operations resulted in a diminution of the supply, but the House of Lords held that the respondent was within his rights in that the acts done were all upon his own land and the interference with the flow of water was an interference with underground percolating water and not water flowing in any defined stream. If the neighbouring landowner's act is a lawful one, it is immaterial what his motives may be, in doing so, and cannot render the act unlawful. This case is supported by an earlier one, *South Shields Waterworks Co.* v. *Cookson* (1845) 15 L.J. Ex. 315, which decided that although there may be a local Act empowering water undertakers to provide water supplies for the local inhabitants, this did not prevent the owners and occupiers of land within the undertakers' limits of supply from sinking wells although the effect might be to draw off water from the undertakers' springs.

It will, however, be appreciated that discussion regarding most of the above decisions is now largely academic, since under the Water Resources Act, 1963 (1) the majority of underground abstractions require the prior licence of the water authority; (2) through the doctrine of "derogation of protected rights" that Act has radically altered the remedies available to an abstractor who is injured through his neighbour's underground activities. An injured party who is entitled to a protected right within the meaning of s.26 of the 1963 Act can bring a civil action for damages against the water authority (not against anyone else) for breach of the statutory duty imposed on the authority under s.29 (2).

Lastly, any commentary on the law regarding underground water would not be complete without some reference to the pollution of percolating water and what rights there may be to the support of underground water.

Pollution of Percolating Water

Although the abstraction or diversion of percolating water is not actionable, the pollution of water trickling through the soil in unknown or undefined channels is actionable, this being an exception to the rule in *Chasemore* v. *Richards.*

In *Hodgkinson* v. *Ennor* (1863) 27 J.P. 469, the plaintiff owned a mill and had an immemorial right to the flow of a stream from a cavern fed by rainwater from underground passages. The defendant owned a mine and discharged polluted water which eventually mingled with the water flowing through the cavern. It was argued for the defendant that under *Chasemore* v. *Richards* no action would lie for interference with underground percolating water, but the court held, following *Tenant* v. *Goldwin* (1703) Holt 500, that an action for fouling the stream was maintainable by the plaintiff. This was followed by *Womersley* v. *Church* (1867) 17 L.T. 190, where an occupier of land was restrained from using a cesspool therein in such a manner as to pollute water coming through his property and supplying a well in adjoining land.

The position was further examined in *Ballard* v. *Tomlinson* (1885) 49 J.P. 692, where the plaintiff and defendant owned adjoining wells and the defendant turned domestic sewage into his well and thus polluted the water which percolated underground from his well to the defendant's property, and consequently polluted water came into the plaintiff's well by pumping. The Court of Appeal held that the plaintiff had a right of action against the defendant for so polluting the source of supply, although the plaintiff had appropriated it he had no property in the percolating water under his land and despite his appropriating the water by the artificial means of pumping.

Some control over the pollution of water underground is afforded by s.31 of the Control of Pollution Act, 1974, which makes it an offence for a person to cause or knowingly permit poisonous, noxious or polluting matter to enter a specified aquifee.

Support from Underground Water

A landowner has no right at common law to the support of underground water. Where a landowner by excavations drained adjoining land so that the soil subsided and cottages thereon became thereby cracked and damaged, the court decided that whilst " a man has no right to withdraw from his neighbour the support of adjacent soil — see *New Moss Colliery* v. *Manchester Corporation* (1908) 72 J.P. 169 — there is nothing at common law to prevent his draining the soil, if for any reason it becomes necessary or convenient for him to do so." But this case has been held not to apply where, along with the withdrawal of underground percolating water from neighbouring land, wet sand and running silt is drawn off, the silt and sand always greatly predominating over the water: *Jordeson* v. *Sutton, Southcoates & Drypool Gas Co.* (1889) 63 J.P. 692.

THE MEDIUM FILUM RULE

Questions of ownership, fishery limits and civic boundaries are determined by this simple legal presumption.

The expression *"ad medium filum viae* (or *aquae*)"* refers to an imaginary line in the middle of a road or river and the *medium filum* rule is a rule of construction at common law that, where a property is bounded on one side or the other by a highway or river, the presumption arises that half the soil of the road or half the bed of the river belongs to the owner of the property, unless there are circumstances to rebut the presumption: *Mickelthwait* v. *Newlay Bridge Co.* (1886) 51 J.P. 132. The rule has been applied in particular to (1) highways, (2) rivers, (3) fisheries, and (4) civil boundaries; it does not apply to a railway which is a boundary: *Thompson* v. *Hickman* (1907) 96 L.T. 454.

As regards highways, the general presumption at law is that the property in the soil of a road belongs *usque ad medium filum viae* to the adjoining proprietors: *Cooke* v. *Green* (1823) 11 Price 736, and this rule applies equally to streets in a town as to roads in the country (*Re White's Charities, Charity Commissioners* v. *London Corporation* (1898) 78 L.T. 550), to both private and public roads (*Holmes* v. *Bellingham* (1859) 23 J.P. 503) and the tenure of the adjoining land, whether freehold or leasehold, is immaterial: *Doe d. Pring* v. *Pearsey* (1827) 7 B. & C. 304. Where there is a conveyance of land abutting on a highway, it is presumed that the conveyance passes half the soil of the road, unless there is sufficient in the circumstances or enough in the expression of the instrument to show that this is not the intention of the parties (*Mickelthwait* v. *Newlay Bridge Co., supra*), even though reference is made to a plan annexed and the measurement and colouring exclude the highway: *Berridge* v. *Ward* (1861) 25 J.P. 695. The presumption may be rebutted on proof of sufficient evidence that the soil in the highway is not vested in the owners of adjoining premises: *Beckett* v. *Leeds Corporation* (1872) 36 J.P. 596.

In the case of rivers, the presumption exists that a person whose land abuts on a watercourse owns the bed of the watercourse up to the middle of the stream and, if he owns the land on both sides, the whole bed of the river belongs to him: *Blount* v. *Layard* (1891) 2 Ch. 681. This presumption does not arise in respect of canals (*Chamber Colliery Co.* v. *Rochdale Canal Co.* [1895] A.C. 564), tidal waters (*R.* v. *Trinity House* (1662) 1 Sid. 86), or where the river bed and the adjoining land are in different ownerships. There is some doubt whether the rule is applicable to large lakes having a number of riparian owners; *Marshall* v. *Ulleswater Steam Navigation Co. Ltd.*, (1863) 3 B. & S. 732; *Johnston* v. *O'Neill* [1911] A.C. 552. On non-tidal rivers the presumption is that the right of fishing is in the several riparian owners *ad medium filum aquae* and, if the same person is the owner of both banks, he has the entire fishing to the extent of the length of his land: *Tracey Elliot* v. *Morley (Earl)* (1907) 51 S.J. 625.

No decisions have been given in the English courts as to how the middle line of a river is to be determined, but it has been suggested (Stuart Moore's *History and Law of Fisheries* (1903) pp. 114-118) by reference to the case of *Hindson* v. *Ashby* (1896) 60 J.P. 484 that the *filum* of the bed of a non-tidal river is to be ascertained by taking the middle line of the river at the ordinary and average state of the river. It would also seem that the *medium filum* of a tidal river is halfway between the low water mark of ordinary tides on each side of the river *(Stuart Moore, supra, p. 118).*

The *medium filum* rule also operates in connexion with civil boundaries defined along rivers. Where two parishes are separated by a river, the *medium filum* is the presumptive boundary between them (*R.* v. *Landulph (Inhabitants)* (1834) 1 Mood. & R. 393 N.P.) and, where a parish comes down as far as the banks of a river, there is a *prima facie* presumption that the parish extends as far as the middle of the river: *MacCannon* v. *Sinclair* (1859) 23 J.P. 757. In the case of riparian county boundaries it was decided in *R.* v. *Brecon (Inhabitants), Re Glasbury Bridge* (1850) 14 J.P. 655, that, in the absence of any words in a statute determining the boundary, the ordinary rule of *medium filum aquae* must apply, and the middle of the river continuously was the boundary line between two counties.

LAKE LAW

Bodies of standing water have, legally speaking, much in common with rivers, although there exist certain points of difference.

Much has been said in preceding chapters on the law relating to rivers and flowing water, but little or nothing about the judicial nature of static, standing, or stagnant water in the shape of lakes, ponds and pools.

To begin with, what is meant by a lake? An average dictionary definition gives "an extensive body of water surrounded by land." Ponds and pools are merely smaller variants of lakes. Apparently neither the courts nor statute law have found it necessary to set limits to the word "lake," although *Angell on Watercourses* pointed out that a lake did not lose its distinctive character by reason of its having a river for an outlet, which caused a current for a certain distance towards the outlet. In *Mackenzie* v. *Banks* (1878) 3 A.C. 1324 H.L., it was held that two lakes connected by a narrow and shallow channel, but divided by a causeway of loose stones, were separate and distinct lakes, owing to the difference of name, the configuration of the ground, and the existence of the causeway. "Lake" under s. 13(13) of the Countryside Act, 1968, includes any expanse of water other than a river or canal.

As a general principle there appears to be no major distinction between the law applying to non-tidal rivers and that pertaining to inland non-tidal lakes, at any rate so far as ownership of the soil and bed, navigation, and fisheries are concerned. But the doctrine of accretion has no application in respect of non-flowing water such as lakes or ponds: *Trafford* v. *Thrower* (1929) *The Times,* May 31. The leading cases on lakes are *Marshall* v. *Ulleswater Steam Navigation Co.* (1863) 27J.P. 516; *Bristow* v. *Cormican* (1878) 3 A.C. 641, H.L.; and *Johnston* v. *O'Neill* [1911] A.C. 552.

In *Marshall* v. *Ulleswater,* concerning the Lake District, the plaintiff was held to be the owner of the soil of the lake by reason of a grant to him of a several and exclusive right of fishing in the lake, but the court was in some doubt whether the soil of lakes, like that of fresh-water rivers, belonged *prima facie* to the riparian owners, or whether it vested in the Crown by virtue of the royal prerogative. But the House of Lords in *Bristow* v. *Cormican* decided that the Crown had no *de jure* right to the soil or fisheries of large inland non-tidal lakes such as Lough Neagh in Ireland, although still leaving in doubt the point whether the soil and bed of large navigable lakes belonged presumably to the adjacent owners *ad medium filum aquae*, which is the position as regards non-tidal rivers. (In an earlier Irish case — *Bloomfield* v. *Johnson* (1868) Ir. 8 C.L. 89 — it had been held that a grant from James I, the owner of the lake, of land adjacent to the lake, did not pass the soil of the lake *ad medium filum*).

A later decision by the House of Lords in *Johnston* v. *O'Neill* finally resolved all doubts by stating that the Crown was not of common right entitled to the soil or water of Lough Erne, an inland non-tidal lake, and that this principle applied irrespective of the size of the lake. As the Crown's interest in the beds of lakes is now ruled out (except in cases where the Crown owns land), it appears that the soil and bed of lakes belong to the owners of the adjacent banks *ad medium filum*.

Johnston v. *O'Neill* also decided that the public have no right to fish in lakes and ponds and, presumably the exclusive right to fish in such waters belongs to the riparian owners to the middle line. (*Marshall* v. *Ulleswater, supra*). If a lake is in one ownership *prima facie* the right of fishing is vested in the owner (*Clarke* v. *Mercer* (1859) 1 F. & F. 492). It makes no difference whether the lake is navigable or not. Some of the Broads, *e.g.*, Wroxham and Hickling Broads, have been held to be non-tidal and therefore not open to the public for fishing: *Blower* v. *Ellis* (1886) 50 J.P. 326; *Mickelthwait* v. *Vincent* (1892) 67 L.T. 225.

No right exists at common law for the public to navigate on large lakes, although rights of navigation may arise from dedication or immemorial user, or by statute (*see Marshall* v. *Ulleswater*). Nor is there any authority for saying that a lake on private grounds, touched at one point only by a public road, is subject to a right which makes it a highway by persons launching boats from the highway and boating on it for pleasure: *Bourke* v. *Davis* (1889) 62 L.T. 34.

Where two persons are joint owners of a lake, with a common right of sailing, fishing, floating timber, etc., such right is held not to be indivisable, and either of the persons may convey the whole or any part of his right, even where it is merely appurtenant to the land, provided that the conveyance does not deprive the co-owner of the full enjoyment of his moiety. A co-owner may maintain an action for the regulation of his moiety as he could if there had been no alienation: *Menzies* v. *Macdonald* (1856) 2 Macq. 463.

The provisions of the Control of Pollution Act, 1974, are expressly excluded from being applied to lakes and ponds which do not discharge to a stream (*vide* s.56(1) of the Act) but various statutes contain sections making it an offence to pollute ponds, *e.g.,* s.20 of the Cemetaries Clauses Act, 1847; s.68 of the Public Health Act, 1875; *see* also ss.30, 259 of the Public Health Act, 1936. If a lake becomes polluted, an owner has available the same common law remedies as has a riparian owner in the case of a river.

Facilities, such as sailing, boating, bathing, fishing and other forms of recreation, may be provided for the public on a lake which is a waterway in a national park or country park (National Parks etc. Act 1949, s.13; Countryside Act, 1968, ss.8, 12, 13).

DISCHARGES TO RIVERS

The enjoyment of river water exists either in its removal for public supply, industry, agriculture, etc., or in its use within the channel for fishing, navigation, recreation and so forth. A further benefit of a river is its potention as a depository for effluents and waste water, provided that neither water pollution nor flooding is occasioned.

The flow of water in a river is made up and maintained by both surface water, *i.e.* tributaries and feeder streams, and ground water percolating through the bed and banks. Additionally, the flow may be assisted by a number of artificial discharges to the river in the nature of (1) sewage effluents; (2) trade effluents; and (3) surface water flows, and it is these which are now considered.

Sewage Effluents

The responsibility for providing adequate sewerage facilities rests with the water authorities into whose hands the functions of sewerage and sewage disposal passed from local authorities (subject to the local authorities accepting the agency arrangements as regards sewerage only) on April 1, 1974, under the Water Act, 1973. The water authorities must provide public sewers necessary for effectually draining their districts and deal effectually with the contents of their sewers by means of sewage disposal works or otherwise (Water Act, 1973, s.14(1)). Water authorities are given powers to construct and maintain sewers and to purchase or erect sewage disposal works (see ss. 15-24 of the Public Health Act, 1936). The term "sewage" has not been legally defined, but ss. 22 and 34 of the Act of 1936 refer to both surface water drainage (that is, water draining from roofs and highways) and foul water drainage, being soil sewage and domestic refuse water; the term does not apply to trade wastes which are considered later.

The sewage is conveyed from its various points of origin through the sewers, either by pumping or gravity, to the sewage disposal works, where it is subjected to a series of treatment processes (screening, settlement, filtration, humus tank treatment, etc.) so that the final effluent attains a quality satisfactory for discharge to a convenient watercourse without causing pollution or giving rise to a nuisance.

The final products at a sewage works usually consist of sludge and treated sewage effluent. The sludge is disposed of by deposit on land or may be sold for fertilizer. The final sewage effluent is discharged to a watercourse or tidal waters or settled on a convenient area of land for absorption.

A sewage effluent discharged to a stream has to satisfy a number of legal requirements. Firstly, s.30 of the Public Health Act, 1936, requires that the outfall conveying the effluent to the stream shall not be constructed or used until the effluent has been so treated as not to affect prejudicially the purity and quality of the water in the stream. This requirement is met in practice by the treatment of sewage already described. There have been a number of cases on the earlier provision which s.30 of the Act of 1936 replaced, namely, s.17 of the Public Health Act, 1875. *Durrant* v. *Branksome U.D.C.* (1897) 61 J.P. 77, decided that a local authority have the right to discharge their sewers into a watercourse provided that the effluent is free from all excrementitious or foul or noxious matter, and that surface water may be so discharged though it carries down sand and silt; but water from a road surface charged with black and oily mud constitutes "filthy water" within the meaning of s.17: *Dell* v. *Chesham U.D.C.* (1921) 85 J.P. 186. Where sewage or other filthy water is conveyed into an already polluted stream no offence is committed against s.17 unless the stream is thereby made fouler than it was before (*A.-G.* v. *Birmingham, Tame and Rea District Drainage Board* (1910) 74 J.P. 57) — but today this would not be a good defence to proceedings taken under s.31 of the Control of Pollution Act, 1974. In *A.-G* v. *Ringwood R.D.C.* (1928) 92 J.P. 65, it was held that s.17 was contravened if the purity and quality of the water in a stream was deteriorated at the point of discharge of a sewer, and it is not necessary to show deterioration to the stream in general.

Secondly, by s.31 of the Public Health Act, 1936 (which largely replaced s.19 of the Public Health Act, 1975) water authorities must discharge their functions (*inter alia*) of disposing of sewage so as not to create a nuisance. Decisions given upon the earlier provision held that negligence must be proved in actions alleging a breach of duty under that section (*see Hawthorn Corporation* v. *Kannuluick* (1906) 93 L.T. 644; *Hammond* v. *St. Pancras Vestry* (1876) 38 J.P. 456; *Stretton's Derby Brewery Co.* v. *Derby Corporation* (1894) 69 L.T. 791), although a remedy might lie by way of complaint to the Minister under s.299 of the Act of 1875 and payment of compensation under s.308 of the same Act (*see* now ss. 278 and 322 of the Act of 1936): *Dent* v. *Bournemouth Corporation* (1897) 66 L.J.Q.B. 395; *Hesketh* v. *Birmingham Corporation* (1924) 88 J.P. 77.

Thirdly, section 32 of the Control of Pollution Act, 1974, must be considered in relation to sewage effluents. This is discussed later.

Quite apart from statutory provisions, a local authority (now the water authority) who discharge impure sewage from their sewerage system into a stream and pollute it are liable to an action at common law for damages and will be restrained by injunction from discharging further matter: *Jones* v. *Llanrwst U.D.C.* (1911) 75 J.P. 68; *Haigh* v. *Deudraeth R.D.C.* (1945) 110 J.P. 97. This is based on the principle that a riparian owner is entitled to the water of his stream in its natural flow, without sensible diminution or increase and without sensible alteration in its character or quality, and that any invasion of this right causing actual damage or calculated to found a claim which may ripen into an adverse right entitles the injured party to the intervention of the courts: *Young & Co.* v. *Bankier Distillery Co.* [1893] A.C. 691; *Pride of Derby Angling Association Ltd.* v. *British Celanese, Ltd.* [1953] 1 All E.R. 179; 117 J.P. 52.

Trade Effluents

Substantial quantities of liquid wastes arising from industrial works, factories and trade premises are disposed of variously, *e.g. (a)* by treatment and return to the factory for re-use; *(b)* by discharge (after treatment where necessary) to a convenient watercourse; *(c)* by discharge (after treatment where necessary) to public sewers; *(d)* by discharge to tidal waters.

The discharge of trade effluents to public sewers is governed by the provisions of the Public Health (Drainage of Trade Premises) Act, 1937 as amended by the Public Health Act, 1961, Part V: the Water Act, 1973, ss. 14, 40, sch. 8, para. 76, sch. 9; and the Control of Pollution Act, 1974, ss. 43-45, 108, sch. 3 paras. 8, 18, sch. 4, and it will suffice here to state that all trade effluents must be discharged from trade premises into a public sewer of a water authority *(a)* with the conditional or unconditional consent of the water authority given after the authority have been served with a trade effluent notice, or *(b)* by agreement between the water authority and the trader. Once trade effluent has entered the sewer it mixes with the sewage effluent and is treated at the sewage disposal works and is ultimately discharged to a watercourse in the form of treated sewage effluent.

Trade effluents dispatched direct to a stream with or without prior treatment (this depends on the type, volume and strength of the particular waste) require consent from the water authority under the Control of Pollution Act, 1974 (discussed hereafter), and the discharge of certain trade wastes to watercourses is either restricted or prohibited under statute, *e.g.* s. 68 of the Public Health Act, 1875, as regards gas waste products.

Control of Pollution Act, 1974.

Section 32 of the Control of Pollution Act, 1974, enacts that no person shall without the consent of the water authority cause or knowingly permit any trade or sewage effluent to be discharged into (1) a stream, or the sea within three nautical miles from the coast, such other parts of the territorial sea adjacent to Great Britain as are prescribed by regulations and any other tidal waters in Great Britain; or (2) from land in Great Britain through a pipe into the sea outside the sea and tidal water mentioned in (1) above; or (3) from a building or from plant on to or into any land or into any lake or pond which does not discharge into a stream. Applications for consent must be advertised in newspapers and any written representations are considered. The authority's consent must not be unreasonably withheld and may be granted subject to such conditions as the authority may reasonably impose, including conditions as to the nature and composition, temperature, volume or rate of discharge of effluent, and as to the point of discharge into the stream or the construction or use of the outlet.

A right of appeal lies to the Secretary of State for the Environment on any question as to whether the water authority have unreasonably withheld their consent or as to the reasonableness of any conditions imposed. Should the water authority fail to give consent within three months of an application to them, consent is deemed to have been refused.

For the purposes of the Act of 1974, "sewage effluent" includes any effluent from a water authority's sewage disposal or sewerage works, and "trade effluent" includes any liquid (either with or without particles of matter in suspension) discharged from premises used for carrying on any trade or industry, other than surface water and domestic sewage and any premises wholly or mainly used (whether for profit or not) for agricultural or horticultural purposes or for scientific research or experiment are deemed to be premises used for carrying on a trade (compare this with the definition of "trade effluent" given in s.14(1) of the Public Health (Drainage of Trade Premises) Act, 1937 as amended).

Surface Water Drainage

Surface water collected in sewers from roofs and highways, etc., is as a rule discharged direct to near-by ditches and watercourses, and does not proceed to sewage disposal works, except in districts where the "combined system" of sewerage is employed, *i.e.* one lot of sewers conveying both foul and surface water drainage to sewage disposal works, as against the "separate system" comprising two sets of sewers, one for foul drainage connecting to the disposal works, the other for surface water discharged without any form of treatment to watercourses. Excess storm-water overflows may also discharge direct to watercourses.

What is the legal position regarding the discharge of surface water to streams? A landowner has an unqualified right to drain his land for agricultural purposes in order to get rid of mere surface water, the supply of the water being casual and its flow following no regular or definite course, and a neighbour cannot complain that he is thereby deprived of such water which otherwise would have come to his land: *Rawstron* v. *Taylor* (1855) 11 Ex. 369; *see* also *Greatrex* v. *Hayward* (1853) 8 Ex. 291; *Broadbent* v. *Ramsbotham* (1856) 11 Ex. 602; *Weeks* v. *Heward* (1862) 10 W.R. 557; *Bartlett* v. *Tottenham* (1932) 1 Ch. 114. It is lawful for persons to drain their lands and let the water run into a stream though the result is to swell the water more, particularly at times, than it would have been but for that drainage: *Durrant* v. *Branksome U.D.C., supra.* In a Canadian case, *Groat* v. *Edmonton City* [1927] 2 D.L.R. 886, it was held that every riparian proprietor has the right at common law to drain surface water from his land into any natural watercourse accessible to him, and if such proprietors exercise their rights reasonably, whether they do so individually or collectively, they are not concerned with the effects thereby produced lower down the stream. The water authorities charged with the duty of effectually draining their areas under Part II of the Public Health Act, 1936, are entitled to discharge surface water into a stream so long as the water discharged is not polluted: *Durrant* v. *Branksome U.D.C., supra.*

In addition to sewerage authorities discharging surface water drainage (and treated sewage effluents) to watercourses, housing authorities under the Housing Acts, development corporations under the New Towns Acts, local authorities providing housing accommodation outside their own districts to relieve congestion and over-population under the Town Development Act, 1952, and other large scale developers, both public and private, require to dispose of surface water into adjoining streams.

The provision of big housing estates and industrial development since the 1939-1945 war has given rise in many instances to a problem which relates to the additional surface water resulting from such developments. The construction of houses, other buildings and roads increase the impermeable area in the catchment basin of the watercourse to which the surface water is drained, with the result that both the volume and rate of run-off of the surface water is substantially increased. If the existing watercourse is inadequate to take the increased and accelerated drainage discharged to it, flooding will result downstream and may cause damage to agricultural land and residential property.

Before 1952, the general position was that nobody erecting houses or discharging surface water into a stream could be held liable for any damage caused to a lower riparian owner as a result of flooding due to an increased discharge of surface water to the stream. So far as local authorities were concerned, they relied upon the general rule laid down in *Hestketh* v. *Birmingham Corporation, supra*, that a local authority is liable for misfeasance but not for non-feasance.

However, Denning, L.J., in giving judgment in the Court of Appeal in *Pride of Derby Angling Association Ltd* v. *British Celanese, Ltd.* [1953] 1 All E.R. 179; 117 J.P. 52, stated at p.202 of the former that the distinction between misfeasance and non-feasance was valid only in the case of highways repairable by the public at large and did not apply to any other branch of law. He referred to the *Hesketh* case and said "I fear, for once, Homer nodded. It would, I think, be very unfortunate if the exemption for non-feasance was extended to local authorities generally." He instanced other cases (putting highway cases on one side) where public authorities had been held liable for non-feasance, namely: — *Yielding* v. *Fay* (1594) Cro Eliz 569; *Henley* v. *Lyme Corporation* (1828) 5 Bing 91; *Baron* v. *Portslade Urban District Council* (1900) 64 J.P. 675; *Simon* v. *Islington Borough Council* (1943) 107 J.P. 59.

He went on to say that when a local authority take over or construct a sewage and drainage system which is adequate at the time to dispose of the sewage and surface water for their district, but which subsequently becomes inadequate owing to increased building which the local authority cannot control, and for which they have no responsibility, the local authority are not guilty of the ensuing nuisance. They do not create it nor do they continue it merely by doing nothing to enlarge of improve the system and the only remedy of the injured party is to complain to the Minister of Housing and Local Government under s.322 of the Public Health Act, 1936. In *Glossop* v. *Heston & Isleworth L.B.* (1879) 44 J.P. 36 and *A.-G* v. *Dorking Guardians* (1882) 46 L.T. 573 (which cases had been referred to earlier on the *Pride of Derby* proceedings) the local authority had not themselves constructed the sewers and had only taken them over from others and done nothing. In *Robinson* v. *Workington Corporation* (1897) 61 J.P. 164 and *Hesketh* v. *Birmingham Corporation, supra* (being other cases previously mentioned), the local authority had themselves constructed a drainage system which was quite sufficient at the time, but later became inadequate through increased building which the local authority could not control. But it was very different when the local authorities themselves do the increased building, or permit it to be done, *e.g.* under the Town and Country Planning Acts, because they are then themselves guilty of the increase. They knew, or ought to have known, that the increase in building would cause the existing sewers to overflow and yet they allow it to go on without enlarging the capacity of the sewage system. By doing so, they are helping to fill the system beyond its capacity and are guilty of the nuisance; this being established by *Hawthorn Corporation* v. *Kannuluik, supra,* and *Hanley* v. *Edinburgh Corporation* (1913) 77 J.P. 233. The "non-feasance cases" (*i.e. Yielding* v. *Fay, supra,* etc.), have little or no application today. In the nineteenth century local authorities had no authority over increased building; they neither built houses themselves nor controlled building by others, and anyone who built a house had a statutory right to connect it to the sewer. But the position had altered radically in the last few years, since local authorities had built more houses than anyone else and have full control under planning over the building in their district. The cannot now disclaim responsibility for increased building.

Subsequently, the court in *Smeaton* v. *Ilford Corporation* [1954] 1 All E.R. 923 at p.932; 118 J.P. 290 did not apply Denning, L.J.'s dictum and (1) followed the *Workington* case and decided that s.31 of the 1936 Act absolved the local authority, in the absence of negligence, from liability for the escape of sewage from their overloaded sewers (built and maintained by the local authority) on to the plaintiff's property, and (2) excluded the application of the principle of *Rylands* v. *Fletcher* (1868) L.R. 1 Ex. 265, thus following *Hammond* v. *St. Pancras Vestry, supra,* and *Stretton's Derby Brewery Co.* v. *Derby Corporation, supra* (which established that a local authority are not liable for the escape of sewage from their overloaded sewers, provided they have acted properly in the exercise of their statutory powers and have not been negligent).

The existing state of the law in this aspect may, perhaps, be summed up by saying that the distinction between non-feasance appears not to be material where the cause of action is based on nuisance, although non-feasance may be significant so far as negligence is concerned. Such distinction in relation to the liabilities of inhabitants as respects the repair of the highway expired under s.1 of the Highways (Miscellaneous Provisions) Act, 1961.

COMMON LAW ON THE THAMES

This heading is included as a legal case-study of an individual river. No doubt research on other rivers would reveal a wealth of case-law illustrating their particular history and habits, but, to my mind, the Thames is unique in our national heritage.

The River Thames has made many modest but nevertheless substantial contributions to those branches of the common law concerned with water in its various aspects. This is hardly surprising since the Thames has from time immemorial been one of the major national highways, and its waters have served public and private uses for a similar period.

The Thames has been the subject-matter, or at least the *locus in quo*, of legal decisions in one way or another since the English legal system was first forged, but either the early cases are now too ancient to be regarded as worth-while precedents, or they were not reported or remain buried in old reports and year books written in the Norman-French or other doggerel of their day. Such cases dealt mainly with disputes and claims over fisheries, mill-rights, weirs, rights on the foreshore, franchises of wrecks, etc.

The cases which are referred to here are by no means a complete list of decisions concerning the Thames, nor are they necessarily the most important. They have been chosen on the basis that they help to illustrate the history of this royal and noble river, and indicate the diversity of riparian topics and maritime interests. But first a few words on the early government of the Thames.

Long before any local authorities acquired an interest in the river and before any public bodies were established to supervise its navigation, the Crown by virtue of the royal prerogative as conservator of all ports, havens, rivers, etc., and as protector of the navigation thereof, exercised a vague but imperial control over the Thames and other great rivers of England. Evidence of this is given in a variety of ancient laws dating from 1215 onwards, directing the removal of weirs and other obstacles which hindered the navigation.

63

The conservancy of the Thames from Staines down to the seaward limits was granted by the Crown to the Corporation of London in (reputedly) 1197, and it remained in the hands of the City until 1857, when the modern Thames Conservancy (which continued under that title but with variations in jurisdiction until 1974) was established. It is surprising that over that long period only a few cases on the rights of the City concerning the Thames were reported. *Fazakerley* v. *Wiltshire* (1720) 1 Str. 462, confirmed the right of the City to appoint porters on the river, not only within the City, but also from Staines Bridge to London Bridge and downwards as far as Yandal in Kent. The Corporation also featured in *R.* v. *Smith* (1780) 2 Douglas K.B. 441, where the City fathers were obstructed in making a horse-towing path along the Thames. About 40 years later the City, although conservators and owners of the soil between high and low water mark, were held not to be entitled to grant a licence for the erection of a wharf which caused inconvenience to the public navigation: *R.* v. *Lord Grosvenor* (1819) 2 Starkie 511. A few years after this the City were concerned in another case — *R.* v. *Montague* (1825) 4 B & C. 598 — relating to the various methods of extinguishing public rights of navigation.

So far as the government of the Thames upstream from Staines was concerned, commissioners were made responsible for supervising parts of the Upper Thames in 1605 and again in 1624, and commissions were appointed in 1695, 1751, and 1771 to maintain and improve the whole navigation between Staines and Cricklade. The Upper Navigation Commissioners, as they were known, constructed many of the early locks and weirs, and their functions were transferred to the Thames Conservancy in 1866. There were at least two cases which involved the Upper Commissioners; *Bulbrook* v. *Goodere* (1765) 3 Burr. 1768, in which it was established that the conservancy of the river between Staines and the head of the river was at that time vested in the Crown, and *Provis* v. *Gibbons* (1825) (unreported), which concerned charges prescribed for vessels using locks under the Thames and Isis Navigation Act, 1751.

Some early cases to do with the Thames were concerned not unnaturally, with the navigation. In *Hind* v. *Manfield* (1614) Noy 103, the defendant was fined £200 for diverting part of the river "by which he weakened the current of the river to carry barges, etc., towards London and other houses of the King upon that river; such a thing cannot be done without an *ad quod damnum*, because the river is a highway and diversion could only be effected by patent of the King." Nearly 100 years later, the Crown filed an information against one Clark for building locks on the Thames to the obstruction of navigation; it being affirmed that hindering the course of a navigable river was against Magna Charta *c.* 23: *R.* v. *Clark* (1702) 12 Mod. Rep. 615. Near the end of the same century the question of mooring barges at low water came under consideration in *Wyatt* v. *Thompson* (1794) 1 Esp. 252. Disputes about wrecks and sunken vessels have alwasys been a fruitful source of litigation, and one such case which occurred in the Thames — *Harmond* v. *Pearson* (1808) 1 Camp 515 — decided that the owner of a vessel sunk in a navigable river is bound to place a buoy over the wreck.

Any unauthorized encroachment or invasion of the bed or foreshore of tidal waters by a person who is not the owner, such as the erection of a pier, is known as a purpresture and may be abated by the Crown or the owner. Such actions were formerly quite common and an example is to be found in *A.-G.* v. *Johnson* (1819) 2 Wils. Ch. 87, where the Lord Chancellor granted an injunction *ex parte* on the information of the Attorney-General to restrain a purpresture in the Thames.

It has long been established that the bed and soil of tidal waters are vested in the Crown, and this doctrine has been confirmed in several decisions affecting the Thames: *R.* v. *Trinity House* (1662) 1 Sid. 86 — "the soil in the Thames is the King's; *Bulstrode* v. *Hall* (1663) 1 Sid. 148 — "it is not denied that the soil of all rivers, as far as the flux and reflux of the sea goes, is in the King and not in the lord of the manors without prescription"; *Kirby* v. *Gibbs* (1667) 2 Keble 274 — "by common intendment the lands between high and low water mark belong to the Crown until the contrary appears"; *R.* v. *Smith* (1780) 2 Douglas K.B. 441 — "the right to the soil of a navigable river is not by presumption of law in the owners of the adjoining land, but *prima facie* belong to the King."

The pollution of rivers in England was not very noticeable in the early part of the nineteenth century, but the authorities were even then beginning to take stock of this menace. The evil effects of trade pollution which followed in the wake of the industrial revolution required firm measures to combat them, and this was reflected in *R.* v. *Medley* (1834) 6 C. & P. 292, where a gas company was indicted for a nuisance for discharging gas refuse into the Thames and so destroying fish and rendering the water unfit for drinking.

Steam vessels were using the Thames as early as 1818 and although their numbers, performance, and speed did not then present the problems they do today, it is interesting to note that as far back as 1838 the Corporation of London found it necessary to make a byelaw forbidding steam-boats to be navigated on the Thames at a greater rate than five miles an hour (*vide Tisdell* v. *Combe* (1838) 7 Ad. & El. 788). Two years later when a large steamer collided with a skiff at Woolwich, the occupier of the skiff was drowned and the navigator of the steamer was charged with manslaughter. The court decided (*R.* v. *Taylor* (1840) 9 C. & P. 672) that the navigator was just as responsible for the death as if he had been driving on a public highway on land.

The courts have always resolutely upheld the rights of riparian owners, and in *Rose* v. *Groves* (1843) 7 Jur. 951 they stated that any interference with the right of access which an owner on the banks of a navigable river enjoys to go on the river from any point on his land is actionable without proof of special damage. In *Original Hartlepool Collieries Co.* v. *Gibb* (1877) 41 J.P. 660, concerning a wharf on the Thames, it was established that a riparian owner is entitled to moor vessels of ordinary size alongside his wharf for purposes of loading, etc., at reasonable times and for a reasonable time and even to overlap his premises provided access to adjoining wharves is not disturbed. The owner of the foreshore is said to hold possession of the soil subject to the right of all persons navigating the river to use the waters in all ordinary navigable ways: *A.-G.* v. *Wright* (1897) 77 L.T. 295.

But, conversely, the courts have decided that an owner who improperly obstructs the public navigation by placing structures on the foreshore is responsible for any injury caused thereby: (*Brownlow* v. *Metropolitan Board of Works* (1864) 12 W.R. 871), and the owners of structures on the shores of the Thames may be liable for damage occasioned by negligence unless the structures are kept in repair or notice is given to those using them to the dangers involved: *White* v. *Phillips* (1863) 9 L.T. 388.

About 1840 a dispute arose between the Crown and the Corporation as to which of them was entitled to ownership of the bed and soil of the tidal Thames. The argument, which was apparently not an important one save in principle and benefited only the lawyers engaged, dragged on until 1856, when a compromise was reached. The case did come before the courts (*A.-G.* v. *London Corporation* (1849) 12 Beav. 8, and on appeal (1850) 2 Mac. & G. 247 L.C.), but never reached judgment. The dispute seems to have been one of the principal reasons for the establishment of the modern Thames Conservancy, because once a settlement was reached it was decided that an independent body should be set up for the Thames, and by the Thames Conservancy Act, 1857, the conservancy of the river downstream from Staines, hitherto vested in the Corporation, was transferred to the new board.

The remainder of the navigable Thames between Staines and Cricklade, which had been subject to the Upper Navigation Commissioners since 1771, passed to the Conservators in 1866. The conservancy of the whole Thames remained with the Thames Conservancy until 1908, when the Port of London Authority was created. Then, once again, the river administration was split, the Port Authority taking over the tidal Thames downstream from Teddington Lock, leaving the Conservators in control of the non-tidal part of the river between Teddington and Cricklade. To complete this brief administrative history, it remains to be said that by the Land Drainage Act, 1930, the Thames Conservancy became, in addition to being the navigation authority and a local pollution prevention authority, the drainage board for the Thames above Teddington, giving them jurisdiction for land drainage purposes over the tributaries and principal watercourses discharging to the Thames. Later, under the

River Boards Act, 1948, the Conservancy obtained the equivalent powers of a river board relating to fisheries, and pollution prevention, and then, by the Water Resources Act, 1963, inherited the functions of a river authority so far as water resources was concerned. To bring the story up to date, by order under the Water Act, 1973, the Thames Conservancy passed into the hands of the Thames Water Authority on April 1, 1974.

Reverting to about 1857, one of the functions of the new Conservancy Board was the granting of licences to riparian owners to construct wharves, piers, piles, etc., in or projecting into the river, and before long the courts were called upon to interpret the extent of the Conservators' powers to do so. In *Kearns* v. *Cordwainers Co*. (1859) 23 J.P. 760 it was held that the Conservators were competent to grant a licence for a jetty notwithstanding that it might to some degree obstruct the enjoyment of adjoining owners of the free navigation of the river. But whilst the Conservators' licence might justify the licensee's interference with the public right of navigation, it did not authorize him thereby to affect injuriously the property of other riparian owners: *Lyon* v. *Fishmongers' Co. and Thames Conservators* (1876) 42 J.P. 163; *Lawes* v. *Turner* (1892) 8 T.L.R. 584.

Inherited from the Corporation of London (or so the Conservators thought) was the power to make byelaws for the protection and preservation of fisheries; but the courts determined that the Conservancy had no authority to make byelaws for this purpose, although they could appoint river keepers empowered to enter fishing boats and seize fish illegally taken: *Turnidge* v. *Shaw* (1861) 25 J.P. 294. However, the Conservators subsequently obtained statutory powers to make byelaws for fisheries. Later cases established that the Conservators had no authority to interfere with private rights to fish (*Smith* v. *Andrews* (1891) 65 L.T. 175), and that the public have no rights at common law to fish in the non-tidal Thames, although by the licence, indulgence, or good nature of individual owners they may have been allowed to fish: *Blount* v. *Layard* (1888) 2 Ch. 681.

The primary functions of the Conservators have always been directed towards the maintenance, improvement, and regulation of the navigation, and for these purposes they are empowered by statute to provide and maintain locks, weirs, towpaths, bridges, ferries, landing-stages, etc. The Conservators have no proprietary rights at large in the bed and soil of the river, but they are entitled to exercise their statutory rights; thus, they may dredge — subject to the statutory powers of other bodies: *East London Railway Co*. v. *Thames Conservators* (1904) 68 J.P. 302 — and grant licences for works of navigation irrespective of ownership. In a rating case on river moorings (*Cory* v. *Bristowe* (1877) 2 A.C. 262), they were said to be the proprietors of the bed and soil of the Thames for the purposes of navigation, and to be the owners thereof only for the purposes specified in their Acts: *Thames Conserv-ators* v. *Port of London Sanitary Authority* (1894) 58 J.P. 335.

Navigation apart, one of the Conservators' most important tasks was and still is preventing pollution and maintaining the quality of the Thames water. From their inception, they had the difficult task of stop-ping the early sanitary authorities from discharging crude sewage into the river, particularly above the intakes of the various water undertak-ings supplying water to London. In 1865 the Conservators failed to re-strain the Kingston-on-Thames corporation from draining their sewage into the Thames (*A.-G.* v. *Kingston Corporation* (1865) 29 J.P. 515), but subject to this solitary and temporary failure, by serving notices, taking proceedings and by much urging and persuading, they did eventu-ally oblige the local authorities to carry out remedial measures. There is a long line of cases which gave proof of their determined efforts, *viz: Richmond Vestry* v. *Thames Conservators* (1875) Q.B. (unreported); *R.* v. *Justices of Middlesex* (1881) 45 J.P. 420; *Thames Conservators* v. *Chertsey Rural Sanitary Authority* (1885) 49 J.P. 404; *R.* v. *Staines Local Board* (1888) 53 J.P. 358; *Thames Conservators* v. *Port of Lon-don Sanitary Authority, supra; High Wycombe Corporation* v. *Thames Conservators* (1898) 78 L.T. 463; *Thames Conservators* v. *Gravesend Corporation* (1910) 73 J.P. 381.

Sewage pollution was only part of the broad problem; notices were also served and proceedings taken against a multitude of traders and manufacturers for causing pollution and, in particular, owners of vessels were discouraged from throwing mud and refuse into the river: *Flowers* v. *Raine* (1866) 30 J.P. 135; *Fuller* v. *Payne* (1887) 3 T.L.R. 729.

The Thames, save at its narrowest near the headwaters, has always provided a natural boundary; in early times for tribal heritages and petty kingdoms, and more recently for the administrative shires and counties. The middle of the river is usually accepted as the dividing line (*see*, for instance, *MacCannon* v. *Sinclair* (1859) 23 J.P. 757, but there are many exceptions to this where a portion of a county crosses the river for historical or local reasons.

From time immemorial the public have been entitled to navigate the Thames (a right now confirmed and extended by statute) and it has long been established that the Conservators are under a duty to take reasonable care that persons who pay tolls in respect of vessels navigating the river can navigate without danger — *vide Winch* v. *Thames Conservators* (1872) 36 J.P. 649, where the Conservators were held to be liable for the loss of horses drowned whilst towing a barge, the towpath being defective. In later cases, *Gridley* v. *Thames Conservators* (1886) 3 T.L.R. 108; *Queens of the River Steamship Co.* v. *Thames Conservators and Eastern, Gibb & Co.* (1907) 96 L.T. 901, *Stevens* v. *Thames Conservators* [1958] 1 Lloyds Rep. 401, the Conservators' liability was modified to the extent that their duty was only to take care that the part of the navigation ordinarily used for navigation was safe and did not apply to places, such as wharves, where the navigation could not be said to be going on. Where the duty applied, it must be shown that they knew or ought to have known of the condition giving rise to the danger.

The cases referred to present a fair resemblance to the events and sequences which have occurred on the Thames within the period covered by the growth of the English legal system, but this account falls short of providing a comprehensive picture of the history of the Thames, since the many statutes relating to that river have not been included.

QUERIES OF RIPARIAN OWNERS

People residing alongside a river or having a riparian association often have particular queries or special problems related directly or indirectly to the water.

For the purposes of the above title, riparian owners can be separated into three classes. First, there is the individual who is about to become one, that is to say, the intending purchaser of property who finds that a stream meanders across, or runs alongside the land in question. Then there is the person who has acquired land adjoining a watercourse; it may be that he bought the property incidentally, or specifically because he likes water in connexion with boating, fishing, etc., or wanted to have the stream as an amenity. Thirdly, stands the owner who has purchased the land for the express purpose of profit or business and intends to utilize the water in some way, *e.g.*, he is the owner of a mill with existing water power or his occupation necessitates the abstraction of water for irrigation, industry, farming.

The solicitor acting for the purchaser of a riparian property may wish to make inquiries, directed to ascertaining what benefits or obligations may exist in respect of the presence of the watercourse on or alongside the property being conveyed. It has been recommended from time to time that solicitors acting for the purchasers of riparian land or of land situated in internal drainage districts should make inquiries of the appropriate water authority about particular points or special liabilities affecting the land, such as a financial obligation like a drainage charge, drainage rate, etc., or a licence, consent or order imposing obligations or limiting the use of property.

In addition a purchaser of riparian land or an existing owner of such land often raises questions of the type referred to below.

In the first category of queries fall those concerning the responsibility for maintaining banks and cleansing channels. "AM I UNDER AN OBLIGATION TO REPAIR MY BANK?" A riparian owner or occupier

Any unauthorised and unreasonable interference with the use of is not under any general legal liability to maintain his banks or to keep them in repair (*Hudson* v. *Tabor* (1877) 42 J.P. 20), but a duty to do so may be imposed by statute, *e.g.*, under ss.262 or 264 of the Public Health Act, 1936, under covenant (this may be set out in the title deeds) or by prescription, custom or tenure (*Lyme Corporation* v. *Henley* (1834) 1 Scott 29; *Morland* v. *Cook* (1868) 18 L.T.496; *R.* v. *Baker* (1867) 31 J.P. 692). If no specific liability to repair the banks exists, it is up to the owner or occupier to do so if he wishes to preserve his property, since artificial banks do not last for ever and natural banks are liable to erosion.

"MUST I KEEP THE RIVER CHANNEL CLEAR?" No, a riparian owner is not required to clear the channel from silt and weeds (*Hodgson* v. *York Corporation* (1873) 37 J.P. 725) and in fact he is not even entitled to remove a shoal or natural accretion on the river bed so as to restore the flow of the water to its former state as regards velocity, direction and height: *Withers* v. *Purchase* (1889) 60 L.T. 819). But there are certain statutory provisions which, if applicable, may alter the common law provision, *viz* s.259 of the Public Health Act, 1936, ss. 18, 24 and 26 of the Land Drainage Act, 1976.

If the property is situate on low-lying land, an almost inevitable query is "WILL THE PROPERTY BE SUBJECT TO PERIODICAL FLOODING?" This question usually refers to that part of the property comprising the house, garage and domestic out-buildings, since the average householder is not particularly disturbed if the end of his garden is occasionally gently inundated due to a stream overflowing in times of very bad weather. If the local authority or water authority cannot give definite information on this — and very often they cannot, since their records on this type of data do not always cover individual properties or particular watercourses — it is open to the purchaser's solicitor to raise this as a practical requisition or for the purchaser to make less formal requisitions over a pint in the "local". In some cases the answer will be apparent in the replies given in the local land searches if these reveal that the local planning authority has taken steps *e.g.*, under an operative development plan to restrict building or further building on riverside land affected by flooding. In any event the prudent property owner will see to it that his house insurance covers damage by flood as far as this is practicable.

Coupled with the likelihood of flooding is the inquiry "CAN I RAISE MY BANKS TO PREVENT FLOODING?" An owner is entitled to raise his bank or erect a flood embankment as it becomes necessary to prevent flood water from flowing over his land, but in doing so he must not cause injury to others, if, for instance, the building of flood protection works has the effect of causing the river water to overflow on to property on the opposite bank: *Bickett* v. *Morris* (1866) 30 J.P. 352. But in the case of an extraordinary flood the owner can protect his bank and divert the flood without regard to consequences:*Nield* v. *London & N.W. Railway* (1874) 44 L.J. Ex. 15. *See* also *Gerrard* v. *Crowe* (1921) 124 L.T. 486, where a flood wall was erected some distance away from the banks. Of course, if there were some particular objection or reason why river banks should not be raised, the water authority would no doubt invoke its land drainage byelaws or the local planning authority might intervene.

Next follow a mixture of questions which riparian owners have been known to ask.

"WHAT PROPRIETARY RIGHTS DOES A PURCHASER ACQUIRE WITH A STREAM?" If the stream runs along a boundary, he is presumed at common law to own the bed and soil on his side of the river *ad medium filum fluminis*: *Bickett* v. *Morris, supra.* But this is only a presumption and is liable to be over-ruled by evidence to the contrary. This position is not often expressly set out in the title deeds or marked on any plan annexed to the deeds. If the stream runs through the land so that he owns both banks, he is presumed to be the proprietor of the bed of the whole river within the limits of his property. He is also presumed to own the fishing in his half of the river where it is non-tidal (*Blount* v. *Layard* [1891] 2 Ch. 681), although in many streams the fishing may be non-existent or very coarse. Riparian rights exist by virtue of the ownership of land abutting on a watercourse and are founded on the right of access to the stream and the land must be in actual contact with the stream laterally or vertically: *Stockport Waterworks Co.* v. *Potter* (1864) 10 L.T. 748; *North Shore Railway Co.* v. *Pion* (1889) 61 L.T. 525.

"WHAT RIGHTS EXIST IN RESPECT OF THE BED OF A STREAM?" So far as the bed of a watercourse is concerned, a riparian owner may place erections thereon or otherwise use it so long as he does not interfere with the natural flow of the water or affect the course or width of the channel. In short, he can do what he pleases provided it has no sensible effect on the stream: *A.-G.* v. *Lonsdale* (1868) 20 L.T. 64. But he requires the written consent of the drainage authority under s.28 of the Land Drainage Act, 1976, where the erection or alteration of a mill, dam, weir or other like obstruction is involved, or of the water authority under s. 29 of that Act for a structure in, over or under a main river watercourse. Also an impounding licence is needed under s.36 of the Water Resources Act, 1963, if the water of an inland water is being impeded by a dam, weir or other work. In the case of an existing dam or structure, check that a consent or licence exists. Obstructions must not be placed in the stream which have the effect of throwing back the water on to the land of an upstream proprietor so as to cause damage or flooding: *Saunders* v. *Newman* (1818) 1 B. & Ald. 258. Stakes may be placed in the stream to prevent erosion and cattle pens to stop cattle straying: *Hanbury* v. *Jenkins* (1901) 65 J.P. 631.

"DOES A RIPARIAN OWNER POSSESS ANY RIGHTS IN RES—PECT OF THE WATER ITSELF IN THE STREAM?" The water flowing in a stream does not belong to anybody, but a riparian owner has a right to the enjoyment of the natural stream of water on the surface for his lawful purposes; that is to say, he has a right to have the water come to him in its natural state, in flow, quantity and quality, and to go from him without obstruction: *Chasemore* v. *Richards* (1859) 23 J.P. 596. This right to use the water arises from the right of access to it which the riparian owner possesses by nature and does not come about by his being the owner of the soil of the river bed: *Lyon* v. *Fishmongers' Co.* (1876) 42 J.P. 163. Persons who have a right of access to flowing water may make reasonable use of it; they do not have an exclusive right to the flow of all the water, but only subject to the right of other riparian owners to the reasonable enjoyment of it. Anyone who lawfully abstracts water from a stream has a property in the particular portion of water abstracted, but only during the period of his possession of it: *Embrey* v. *Owen* (1851) 6 Ex. 353.

"IS THERE ANYTHING TO PREVENT A BRIDGE BEING CONSTRUCTED ACROSS A STREAM?" Provided that he owns or has a right of access to both banks, a private individual is at liberty to erect a bridge (subject to any planning or other statutory permission that may be required), so long as the flow is not thereby restricted. Where the stream is main river for the purposes of the Land Drainage Act, 1976, the construction of the bridge must be first approved by the water authority (Land Drainage Act, 1976, s.29). Additionally, if the river is a navigable one, it will usually be necessary to obtain the views of the navigation authority, where the height, width or abutments of the proposed bridge might obstruct or be a danger to the navigation. As to obligations to repair bridges, *see*, in particular s.24 of the Act of 1976.

"WHAT IS THE POSITION ABOUT THE CULVERTING OF WATERCOURSES?" Where a person proposes to build upon land on which a watercourse is situate or abuts, the local authority may by notice require the landowner, before building operations are begun or whilst they are in progress, to fill up the watercourse or to culvert the same. Where the owner himself wishes to culvert, watercourses in urban areas cannot be culverted or covered unless plans have been submitted to and approved by the local authority. The owner or occupier of land in a borough or urban area can be required by the local authority to repair, maintain and cleanse culverts on or under his land (Public Health Act, 1936, ss. 262-264). The culverting or filling in of a watercourse under the jurisdiction of a drainage authority for land drainage purposes requires the approval of the authority.

"WHAT RESPONSIBILITIES DOES A DRAINAGE AUTHORITY HAVE WITH RESPECT TO STREAMS?" The land drainage functions of a water authority or internal drainage board are exercised by reference to certain provisions of the Land Drainage Act, 1976, s.17 of which Act enables the drainage authority to carry out drainage works to watercourses which fall within its jurisdiction. In the case of a water authority these watercourses are usually the major rivers and streams within the water authority area, are referred to as the "main river" and are those shown on the official map of the catchment area prepared and approved by the Minister of Agriculture, Fisheries and Food in accordance with s.9 of the Act of 1976. The powers of the authority to execute drainage works are permissive and not obligatory (*East Suffolk Rivers Catchment Board* v. *Kent* (1941) 105 J.P. 129), but the authority normally carries out any necessary works to the main river from time to time by way of dredging, weed clearance, widening, removing shoals and fallen trees and so on, and in this way relieves the riparian owners of having to do such work for themselves. The authority does not usually accept responsibility for maintaining banks, erecting fencing along the tops of banks or repairing or operating private sluices or weirs. The Act does not vest in authorities the bed and soil of watercourses, which remain the property of the riparian owners; the Act simply empowers authorities to carry out land drainage works to the main river. In addition to land drainage, water authorities possess other functions with regard to watercourses in their areas, being those relating to fisheries, the prevention of pollution, water conservation and, occasionally, navigation.

"HAS AN OWNER ON THE BANKS OF A NAVIGABLE RIVER ANY SPECIAL RIGHTS?" The broad rule is that there is no distinction in principle between riparian rights on the banks of a navigable or tidal river and those of a non-navigable river (*North Shore Railway Company* v. *Pion, supra*), subject to the public right of navigation. Thus, an owner may erect works on the river bed and moor vessels and floating jetties alongside his property, provided the right of navigation is not thereby obstructed: *Orr Ewing* v. *Colquhoun* (1877) 2 A.C. 839): *Booth* v. *Ratte* (1889) 62 L.T. 198. An owner is entitled to a right of access to a navigable river from any point on his banks: *Marshall* v. *Ulleswater Steam Navigation Co.* (1871) 36 J.P. 583. Where a navigation or conservancy authority has been established for a river it is necessary to observe any laws or rules prescribed under the authority's statutes, *e.g.* on the navigable Thames pleasure craft must be registered and river accommodations such as wharves and mooring piles have to be licensed.

"DOES THE PRESENCE OF A TOWPATH ALONG THE BANKS OF A NAVIGABLE RIVER RESTRICT THE RIPARIAN OWNER'S USE OF HIS LAND CROSSED BY THE TOWPATH?" Assuming that the soil of the towpath is not vested in any navigation authority, but in the riparian owner subject only to the right of towing (*see Lea Conserv-ancy Board* v. *Button* (1881) 46 J.P. 164), the owner may use the towpath as he thinks fit, provided no obstruction, interference or injury is caused thereto: *Thames Conservators* v. *Kent* (1918) 83 J.P. 85; which case deals with the position where the towpath is also a public path.

Specialist questions which might concern the keen fisherman, riparian industrialist, or mill owner cannot be dealt with here, but these are a few of the points which might be raised in such circumstances.

"ARE THERE ANY RESTRICTIONS ON ABSTRACTING WATER FROM STREAMS?" Yes, apart from the exceptions mentioned in s.24 of the Water Resources Act, 1963, a licence is required from the water authority. This states the name of the licensee, the quantity of water which can be abstracted per day, per year, the purposes for which the water is to be abstracted, etc.

"CAN SURPLUS WATER BE DISCHARGED TO A WATER—COURSE?" This depends upon the type of water to be discharged. An individual may drain surface water from his land to an adjoining stream (*Durrant* v. *Branksome U.D.C.* (1897) 61 J.P. 77), but discharges liable to cause pollution cannot be conveyed to a stream, since this renders the person responsible liable to a prosecution under s.31 of the Control of Pollution Act, 1974. Any discharge in the nature of a trade or sewage effluent should be connected to the main drainage system where possible, and must be so connected in certain circumstances. Otherwise, trade and sewage effluent will probably have to be discharged to a watercourse after treatment, in which event the consent of the water authority is required under ss. 32 and 34-40 of the Control of Pollution Act, 1974.

"WHAT IS THE POSITION ABOUT WEIRS AND SLUICES WHICH ARE PART OF THE PROPERTY?" It is important for an intending purchaser to ascertain whether he is under any liability (1) to maintain, and (2) to operate, any weirs or sluices which belong to or are sited on the property, as these liabilities can prove expensive by present day standards of prices. The title deeds may be silent on these points, since the works may have been installed by a previous owner many years ago and an obligation as to maintenance and operation may have subsequently been acquired by prescription. Extensive enquiries in the locality might be necessary to discover whether obligations of this nature exist. The position is to some extent governed by statute; under s.24 of the Land Drainage Act, 1976, a person who is under an obligation to repair or maintain a drainage work and fails to do so, may be required to do the necessary work by the drainage authority. Provisions concerning the operation and maintenance of sluices, weirs, dams, etc., are contained in the land drainage byelaws made by water authorities and internal drainage boards. In the absence of an agreement or obligation to keep in repair, it appears that the owner of a dam or weir may permit it to fall into disuse, despite what effects this may have upon upper riparian owners in respect of the fall in normal water level: *Mason* v. *Shrewsbury & Hereford Railway* (1871) L.R. 6 Q.B. 586; but *see* also *Buckley* v. *Buckley* (1892) 67 L.J., Q.B. 953.

"IF THERE IS A WELL ON THE PROPERTY CAN I USE IT FOR DRINKING?" Yes, if the water is suitable. Water abstracted from underground strata by or on behalf of a person as a supply for the domestic purposes of his household is exempt from the requirement of an abstraction licence by virtue of s.24 (3) of the Water Resources Act, 1963. But if the well water is used, e.g. for agriculture, or many other purposes, then a licence is necessary.

"CAN I FISH IN THE RIVER?" Where the owner of the property also has the right of fishery in the river he may fish there. There is a legal presumption that the right of fishery in a non-tidal river is vested in the respective riparian owners up to the middle of the river, but it is always possible that different people own (a) the river bank; (b) the river bed, and (c) the right to fish. If the river is tidal, however, the public are entitled to fish (and navigate) unless the existence of a several fishery can be proved.

THE DOCTRINE OF ACCRETION

The advance or retreat of the sea, or the wearing away of a river channel, results in the seashore or river bank either being added to or eroded. This has attracted the attention of the courts and legal principles have been defined.

Sir Matthew Hale, Lord Chief Justice from 1671 to 1676, in his work *De Jure Maris* stated that the King had title to the increase of land from the sea(*maritima incrementa*), which was of three kinds — (1) increase *per alluvionem* (alluvion) or land washed up by the sea; (2) increase *per relictionem* (dereliction), being derelict land or land left dry by the recess of the sea; (3) increase *per insulae productionem*, where islands or islets are gradually or suddenly formed out of the sea or at the mouths of rivers. Since Hale's day, the legal principles and canons governing the doctrine or rule of accretion have been "gradually and imperceptibly" extended, varied and modified.

The operation of the doctrine does not appear to depend upon the maxim *"De minimis non curat lex"* as is imagined by some, and according to Lindley, J., in *Foster* v. *Wright* (1878) 44 J.P. 7, "the law on this subject (*i.e.* of accretion) is based upon the impossibility of identifying from day to day small additions to or subtractions from land caused by the constant action of running water ... the question does not depend on any doctrine peculiar to the royal perogative." In *Hindson* v. *Ashby* (1896) 60 J.P. 484, it was said that "the whole doctrine of accretion is based on the theory that from day to day, week to week, and month to month a man cannot see where his old line of boundary was by reason of the gradual and imperceptible accretion of alluvium to his land."

Accretion on the Foreshore.

Land which is slowly, gradually and imperceptibly formed on the foreshore from the sea, whether by accretion (alluvion) or by the sea retreating (dereliction), belongs by general immemorial custom to the

77

owner of the adjoining soil and not to the Crown, and, conversely, land gradually encroached upon by water becomes part of the sea. Where the increase is sudden or perceptible, the land gained still belongs to its original owner. "Imperceptible" in this issue, as connected with the words "slow and gradual," must be understood as expressive only in the manner of the accretion, not imperceptible after a long lapse of time: *Gifford* v. *Yarborough(Lord)* (1828) 5 Bing 163, H.L. The recognition of title by alluvial means is largely governed by the fact that the accretion is due to the nominal action of physical forms. In the rule that it must be "gradual, slow and imperceptible," the last two words are only qualifications of the word "gradual," and that word with its qualifications only defines the test relative to the conditions to which it is applied: *Secretary of State for India* v. *Vizianagaram (Raja)* (1921) L.R. 49 Ind. App. 67.

The owner of the shore between high and low water mark is entitled to such parts of the adjoining soil as, by the gradual and imperceptible encroachment of the sea, have been brought within those limits, and the owner of the land next adjoining high water mark is entitled to all the soil that is added to his land by the imperceptible retiring of the sea. The same rule holds with regard to rivers: *Re Hull & Selby Rly.* (1834) 8 L.J. Ex. 260.

The general law of accretion applies to a gradual and imperceptible accretion of land abutting on the foreshore, brought about by the operation of nature, and the rule applies even though it has been unintentionally assisted by, or would not have taken place without, the erection of groynes for the purpose of protecting the shore from erosion: *Brighton & Hove General Gas Co.* v. *Hove Bungalows Ltd.* (1924) 88 J.P. 61. The rule as to accretion is limited to the seashore or land abutting on running water and does not apply to canals, lakes, or ponds: *Trafford* v. *Thrower* (1929) *The Times*, May 30, and applies to the sea and to tidal and non-tidal waters, whether navigable or not: *Foster* v. *Wright, supra*. The title by accretion to a new formation of alluvial land is not generally founded on equity of compensation, but on a gradual accretion by adherence to some particular land; the land so gained follows the title to which it adheres: *Sree Eckowrie Sing* v. *Heeraloll Seal* (1868) 12 Moo. Ind. App. 136.

Until 1924 it was considered doubtful whether the doctrine of accretion applied where the boundaries of land were well defined and known and that it might only operate where there were no fixed boundaries. This doubt was expressed in *Ford* v. *Lacy* (1861) 30 L.J. Ex. 351, and also in *Hindson* v. *Ashby, supra*, where it was stated that, while the doctrine might not apply if the boundary on the waterside is a wall or something so clear and visible that it is easy to see whether the accretions, as they become perceptible, are on the one side of the boundary or on the other, the court was not satisfied that the doctrine was not applicable to the cases of land having no boundary next flowing water, except the water itself. But this point now appears to have been resolved in *Brighton & Hove Gas Co. v. Hove Bungalows Ltd., supra,* where it was decided that the general law of accretion also applied where a natural accretion, gradual and imperceptible, abuts on land of which the former boundary was already well known and readily ascertainable: *see* also *A.-G. v. M'Carthy* [1911] 2 I.R. 260.

In *Mellor v. Walmesley* (1905) 93 L.T. 574, a plot of land mentioned in a conveyance was described as "situate on the seashore." It was held (i) that the "seashore" was the land situate between medium, high and low water marks; (ii) that the land between the plot and the foreshore did not pass to the grantee, but the grantor was estopped from saying that the land beyond the plot was anything but "foreshore"; (iii) that the land in dispute must as between the grantor and the grantee be held to be an accretion subsequent to the conveyance, and accordingly to be land which had become the property of those claiming under the grantee. A conveyance of land bounded by the sea passes the land from time to time added by accretion: *Scratton v. Brown* (1825) 4 B. & C. 458; *see* also *Nesbitt v. Maplethorpe U.D.C.* (1917) 81 J.P. 289. Where the Crown seeks to recover land alleged to have been reclaimed from the sea, if the defendant admits the Crown's title to the foreshore, then upon an inquiry as to what is the boundary of the foreshore, the onus is thrown on the Crown of showing that the high water mark in former times extended further inland than at present: *A.-G. v. Chamberlain* (1858) 4 K. & J. 292. Land gained imperceptibly becomes subject to the legal attributes of the land to which it accretes and may become freehold or leasehold or subject to customary rights: *Mercer v. Denne* (1905) 70 J.P. 65. In the case of a temporary encroachment, the property remains in the owner of the land encroached upon: *Hayes v. Hayes* (1897) 31 I.L.T. 392.

Artificial reclamation and natural silting up are two extremely different things in their legal results; the latter, if gradual and imperceptible, becomes an addition to the property of the adjoining land; the former has not this result, and the property of the original foreshore suddenly altered by reclamatory work upon it remains as before: *A.-G. of Southern Nigeria v. Holt & Co. (Liverpool), Ltd.* [1915] A.C. 599, where land reclaimed by the respondents and not the result of natural accretion was held to be vested in the Crown as owner of the foreshore (in the absence of the respondents being able to prove title against the Crown by showing that they had had possession of the foreshore for 60 years), but the respondents continued to have the right of riparian owners over the foreshore and there was presumed in their favour an irrevocable licence from the Crown to erect buildings and to store goods upon the reclaimed land and to use it generally for the purposes of their business. It was also held that the rule as to accretion applies to all riparian lands even though they may be scheduled to or specifically measured or coloured on a plan in the title deeds.

In *A.-G.* v. *Reeve* (1885) 23 J.P. 308, where accretions of land were due to the erection of harbour works on the seashore carried out under statutory powers and the removal of shingle under licence, and the accretion was preceptible by marks and measures as they took place, it was held that the land gained belonged to the Crown and not to the adjacent owner.

Islands which rise from the sea within the three mile limit of territorial waters are presumed to be the property of the Crown, and the onus of establishing a title by adverse possession lies upon the person asserting such possession: *Secretary of State for India* v. *Chelikani Rama Rao* (1916) L.R. 43 Ind. App. 192.

The principles of the doctrine of accretion arc based on common law, but the doctrine is occasionally affected by statute. Thus, by s.72 of the Local Government Act, 1972, every accretion from the sea, whether natural or artificial, and any part of the seashore to low water mark which did not on October 26, 1972, form part of a parish, is for all local government purposes annexed to and incorporated with the parish or parishes which the accretion or part of the foreshore adjoins in proportion to the extent of the common boundary and is also annexed to and incorporated with the districts and county in which the parish is situate. Section 36 of the Land Drainage Act, 1976, provides that where the Minister of Agriculture, Fisheries and Food certifies that, as the result of drainage works executed or proposed to be executed by a water authority in connexion with the tidal waters of main rivers under the jurisdiction of the authority or drainage works transferred from a drainage authority in pursuance of the Act, there has been or is likely to be an accretion of land, the authority may purchase the accretion of land or the land to which the accretion will if it takes place be added, together with any right to reclaim or embank the accretion of land.

Accretion in Rivers

Alluvial lands which are gradually gained from a river belong by way of accretion to the lands of the adjoining owner: *Mussumat Imam Bandi* v. *Hurgovind Ghose* (1848) 4 Moo. Ind. App. 403. In *Foster* v. *Wright, supra*, a river, then running wholly within the plaintiff's property, afterwards wore away its bank and by gradual progress, which was not visible but periodically ascertained over a period of years, eventually encroached upon the defendant's land until a strip of it, defined and identified, became part of the river. The plaintiff brought an action for trespass against the defendant for fishing on the strip covered by water. The court upheld the action on the grounds that gradual accretions of land from water belong to the owner of the land gradually added to *(Gifford* v. *Yarborough, supra)*; and conversely land gradually encroached upon by water ceases to belong to the former owner *(Hull and Selby Rly., supra)*. Upon this question the court could see no difference between tidal and non-tidal or navigable or non-navigable rivers. But whether a strip of land has ceased to be part of the river is a question to be determined not by any hard and fast rule but by regard to all the material circumstances of the case, including the fluctuations of the river, the nature of the land, and its growth and user: *Hindson* v. *Ashby, supra.*

If the change in the course of a river is sudden and perceptible and if the former marks remained and the extent can be reasonably ascertained, the soil remains in the former owner: *Ford* v. *Lacy, supra.* Where a non-tidal river which separates two estates belonging to different owners suddenly changes its course, the property in the soil does not change: *Thakurain Ritraj Koer* v. *Thakurain Sarfaraz Koer* (1905) 21 T.L.R. 637. If by the irruption of the waters of a tidal river, a new channel is formed in the land of a subject, although the rights of the Crown and of the public may come into existence and be exercised in what has become a portion of the tidal river, the right to the soil remains in the owner, so that if at any time thereafter the waters should recede and the river again change its course, leaving the new channel dry, the soil becomes again the exclusive property of the owner, free from all rights in the Crown and the public: *Carlisle Corporation* v. *Graham* (1869) 21 L.T. 333. Some local Acts contain a provision that, where a riparian owner constructs an embankment in front of his land, then the land reclaimed by the embankment shall vest in the same person and for the same estate and interest as the land in front of which the embankment has been constructed: *see* s. 63 of the Thames Conservancy Act, 1932.

OBSTRUCTION IN RIVERS

The hindrance of navigation and obstructions to the river flow have always concerned the courts which have provided appropriate remedies.

Decisions of the courts over the past two and a half centuries give a wealth of detail concerning the illegality of obstructing the public navigation in rivers. In *R.* v. *Clark* (1702) 12 Mod. Rep. 615, an information was filed against Clark for causing locks to be built on the Thames to the obstruction of the navigation, and it was held that hindering the course of a navigable river and the taking of tolls to let people pass was contrary to the provisions of Magna Carta. The erection of a wharf or other accommodation in a navigable river, even though under licence of the conservancy authority, may be illegal if the wharf produces inconvenience to the public using the river for the purposes of navigation: *R.* v. *Lord Grosvenor* (1819) 2 Starkie 511.

At common law the obstruction of a public navigable river amounts to a public nuisance, and may be the subject of indictment (*R.* v. *Russell* (1827) 6 B. & C. 566), and *prima facie* any structure in the bed of a river may amount to an obstruction, as for instance in *A.-G.* v. *Terry* (1874) 38 J.P. 340, where a wharf, which extended so as to occupy 3 *ft.* out of a breadth of some 60 *ft.* available for navigation, was held to be an obstruction, although it only occurred at certain times of the tide. But whether an obstruction amounts to a nuisance is a question of fact for the jury, who are to say whether the public are in any way inconvenienced (*R.* v. *Bell* (1822) 1 L.J.K.B. 42); there must be actual obstruction: *R.* v. *Betts* (1850) 16 Q.B. 1022; 14 J.P.N. 318. It is no defence to show that an obstruction in a river impeding navigation was not an obstruction at the time it was erected, but has become such because part of the river has silted up, or for some other reason (*Williams* v. *Wilcox* (1838) 8 Ad. & El. 314); nor can an obstruction be excused on the ground that the impediment affords facilities to the public: *Denaby and Cadeby Main Collieries, Ltd.* v. *Anson* (1911) 103 L.T. 349. A right to obstruct a navigable river cannot be acquired by length of time: *Vooght* v. *Winch* (1819) 2 B. & Ald. 662.

A riparian owner may build an erection on his land though covered with water, so long as it does not interfere with the right of navigation, or with the rights of other riparian owners (*Orr Ewing* v. *Colquhoun* (1877) 2 A.C. 839), but obstructions must not be erected in a stream so as to throw back the water on to an upper riparian owner's land so as thereby to flood his land or injure his mill; *Saunders* v. *Newman* (1818) 1 B. & Ald. 258. However, such a right may be acquired as an easement: *Alder* v. *Savill* (1814) 5 Taunt. 454. A natural obstruction or one formed by long natural deposit must not be removed if by doing so an injury would be inflicted on a lower riparian owner: *Withers* v. *Purchase* (1889) 60 L.T. 819.

A river may become obstructed in a variety of ways, *i.e.*, by (1) weirs and dams placed across the river; (2) wharves, piers and other accommodation works projecting into the stream; (3) the channel silting up; (4) ballast and rubbish thrown into the stream; (5) vessels sunk or inconveniently moored; (6) miscellaneous obstacles. It is proposed to discuss quite briefly the legal aspects of these different kinds of obstructions.

Weirs and dams

In early times, when roads were few and poor and movement by water was an important form of transport, there was apt to be bitter dispute, between those who used the rivers for purposes of commerce and navigation and the owners of mills and fisheries whose livelihood demanded streams restricted by mill dams, fish weirs, and the like. The free movement of navigation was encouraged in early statutes in which weirs were regarded as public nuisances. Magna Carta (*c.* 26) declared that "all weirs from henceforth shall be utterly put down through Thames and Medway and through all England, except by the sea coast." This prohibition was repeated in a slightly later law, 9 Hen. III, c. 23 (1225), and a further Act, 25 Ed. III st. 4, c. 4 (1350), (confirmed by 45 Ed. III, c. 2 (1371)) also ordered the destruction of all weirs, mills and other fixed engines of fishing which had been set up in or after the time of Edward I. These provisions were held to relate to navigable rivers only, and did not apply to weirs shown to have been in existence before the time of Edward I: *Williams* v. *Wilcox, supra; Rolle* v. *Whyte* (1868) L.R. 3 Q.B. 286.

During the nineteenth century the improvement of roads and the construction of canals and railways led to a decline in the importance of rivers for navigation, and rivers began more to be regarded from the point of view of fisheries. The position as regards fisheries is regulated at the present time under part II of the Salmon and Freshwater Fisheries Act, 1975, which prohibits the placing of fixed engines or using unauthorized fixed engines for taking or obstructing the free passage of salmon or migratory trout in inland and tidal waters. Unauthorized fishing weirs or fishing mill dams cannot be used for taking such fish, but (*a*) fishing weirs extending more than halfway across a river at the lowest state of water may be used for taking salmon, provided such weirs have a free gap in the deepest part of the river between the points where it is intercepted by the weir, and (*b*) a fishing mill dam may be used to catch salmon if it has attached to it a fish pass approved by the Ministry of Agriculture, Fisheries and Food. A water authority may acquire or take on lease, either by agreement or compulsorily, a dam, fishing weir, fixed engine, or other artificial obstruction, and alter or remove the obstruction, and may, with the Minister's consent, construct a fish pass in a dam and abolish, alter or restore any existing fish pass or free gap.

Section 28 of the Land Drainage Act, 1976, requires that no mill dam, weir or other like obstruction to the flow of a watercourse may be erected, raised or otherwise altered without the written consent (not to be unreasonably withheld) of the drainage authority. Any question arising whether such consent is unreasonably withheld must be referred to arbitration. If any obstruction is erected, etc., in contravention of this provision, it is deemed to be an offence and the authority may serve notice upon the offender requiring him to abate the nuisance within a specified time. In default, the authority can obtain a summons requiring the person to appear before a magistrates' court who, if satisfied that the alleged nuisance exists, may order the person to abate the nuisance and impose a penalty not exceeding £400. Further, the construction or alteration of impounding works, *i.e.* a dam or weir, in an inland water needs a licence to impound from the water authority under s.36 of the Water Resources Act, 1963.

Accommodation works

On an indictment for a nuisance in a navigable river by erecting staiths for loading coal on to vessels it was held that a direction by the Judge to the jury that the erection of the staiths was a public benefit was proper: *R. v. Russell, supra*. But in a later case concerning the erection of a wharf (*R. v. Randall* (1842) Car. & M. 496), it was decided that the question for the jury was whether the wharf occasioned any hindrance to river nagivation by vessels of any description, and not whether the erecting of the wharf had caused a benefit to navigation in general. In *A.-G. v. Terry, supra*, it was said "it is no answer to say that there is room for the ships and that if they are navigated with skill and care there will be no obstruction. Those who use the river are entitled to say that they have a right to the whole of the space."

The general principle is that any one who places or keeps in a navigable river any obstruction to the navigation is liable for injury caused thereby (*Brownlow* v. *Metropolitan Board of Works* (1864) 6 L.T. 187), and the owners of structures on the shores of navigable rivers may be responsible for damage occasioned by negligence unless such structures are kept in repair or the owner gives notice of the danger: *White* v. *Phillips* (1863) 9 L.T. 388. In *Queens of the River Steamship Co.* v. *Thames Conservators* (1907) 96 L.T. 901, a river conservancy authority were held to be under a duty to take reasonable care that persons who pay tolls in respect of vessels navigating the river can navigate without danger; but this duty is only to take care that the part of the river ordinarily used for navigation is safe and does not apply to places where the navigation cannot be said to be going on, such as wharves. Where the duty applies the authority are not liable unless they knew or ought to have known of the condition giving rise to the damage. A conservancy authority who are empowered to remove obstructions in the river are not under a duty to remove piles in part of their navigation for which they are forbidden to collect tolls, although the piles are dangerous and the authority ought to have been aware of the danger: *Forbes* v. *Lee Conservancy Board* (1879) 4 Ex. D. 166.

If a jetty, which obstructs to some degree the public navigation of a river, is constructed under the authority of a statute, no action will lie against the owner of the jetty by adjoining owners alleging that the jetty obstructs their free navigation of the river, since the effect of the statute was to contemplate some interference with the navigation: *Kearns* v. *Cordwainers' Co.* (1857) 23 J.P. 760; *see* also *A.-G.* v. *Thames Conservators* (1862) 8 L.T. 9. But though a statutory licence might be the licensee's justification as far as the public right of navigation is concerned, it does not authorize the licenses thereby to affect injuriously the land of another riparian owner: *Lyon* v. *Fishmongers' Co.* (1876) 42 J.P. 163.

Silting up of channel

There is no liability at common law on the owner of the bed of a navigable river to prevent the navigation from becoming silted up and choked with weeds, although the owner takes tolls for the navigation (*Hodgson* v. *York Corporation* (1873) 37 J.P. 725), and the proprietor of an inland navigation, who was not the owner of the bed, was held not to be under any obligation to cut the weeds or dredge the silt, unless it was necessary to do so for the benefit of the navigation: *Cracknell* v. *Thetford Corporation* (1869) 38 L.J.C.P. 353.

By s.17 of the Land Drainage Act, 1976, water authorities and internal drainage boards are empowered to maintain and improve watercourses, although this is a permissive and not a mandatory function (*East Suffolk Rivers Catchment Board* v. *Kent* (1941) 105 J.P. 129)., and under s.40 of that Act a riparian owner may be compelled to cleanse a ditch if his neglect to do so causes injury to any other land. Section 18 of the Act places the person having control of a watercourse (other than one forming part of a main river) or the riparian occupier under a duty of maintaining the watercourse, so that the proper flow of water is not so impeded.

Under s.259 of the Public Health Act, 1936 any part of a watercourse, not being ordinarily navigated by vessels employed in the carriage of goods by water, which is so choked or silted up as to obstruct or impede the proper flow of water so as to cause a nuisance or give rise to conditions prejudicial to health is regarded as a statutory nuisance for the purposes of part III of the Act. This provision cannot be exercised in respect of a watercourse within the jurisdiction of a drainage authority except after consultation with the board.

Ballast and rubbish thrown into rivers

It is an offence under several statutes to cast ballast, rubbish, etc., into rivers. Section 11 of the Harbours Act, 1814, forbids ballast, rubbish, etc., to be cast or thrown from ships or from the shore into harbours, havens, or navigable rivers (so far as the tide flows) so as to tend to injure or obstruct the navigation. Every person who throws or puts ballast, earth, ashes, stone, or other thing into a dock or harbour is guilty of an offence, unless done for the purpose of recovering land lost by reason of the overflowing or washing of a navigable river or for protecting land from future loss or damage (Harbours, Docks and Piers Clauses Act, 1947, s.73). By s.259 (2) of the Public Health Act, 1936, a person who throws or deposits cinders, ashes, bricks, stone, rubbish, dust, filth or other matter likely to cause annoyance into or in a river, stream or watercourse or who suffers any such act to be done, is liable to a penalty not exceeding £2.

Moored or sunken vessels

The mooring and keeping moored of a vessel across a public navigable creek, thus preventing the plaintiff from navigating his barges and involving him in having to convey his goods a great distance by land, was held in *Rose* v. *Groves* (1843) 5 Man. & G. 613, to be special damage for which an action would lie.

The owner of a vessel sunk by misfortune or accident in a navigable river cannot be indicted for not removing it (*R.* v. *Watts* (1798) 2 Esp. 675), but the owner of a vessel sunk by unavoidable accident in a navigable channel, whether in the usual track of navigation or not, so long as he continues to have possession and control of the vessel, must take due precautions to prevent injury to other vessels by their striking against it: *White* v. *Crisp* (1854) 10 Ex. 312. Power is given under statute for harbour and conservancy authorities to remove or destroy wrecks and to recover the expenses thereby incurred; *see* s.56 of the Harbours, Docks and Piers Clauses Act, 1894, and s.16 of the Thames Conservancy Act, 1950.

Miscellaneous obstacles

A ferry rope (*Hilton* v. *Scarborough (Lord)* (1714) 2 Eq. Cas. Abr. 171), or a mooring anchor, whether floating or under the water, the position of which is insufficiently marked or indicated, may amount to an obstruction: *Jolliffe* v. *Wallasey L.B.* (1873) 38 J.P. 40; *Hancock* v. *York, etc., Rly.* (1850) 10 C.B. 348. A bridge across a navigable river, even if its erection is not authorized, is not necessarily an obstruction (*R.* v. *Betts, supra*), but unreasonable delay in operating a swing bridge can amount to an obstruction: *Wiggins* v. *Boddington* (1828) 3 C. & P. 544. Raising the level of the water in a stream is not usually a proper subject of complaint for the interference of the courts: *Ingram* v. *Morecraft* (1863) 33 Beav. 49. The placing of public services, such as electric cables and telegraph lines, across navigable channels is effected under statute with due safeguards for preventing interference with the navigation (*see* s.22 of the Electricty (Supply) Act, 1919, as amended; ss. 6 and 32 of the Telegraph Act, 1963, as applied by s.2 of the Telegraph Act, 1868, etc). It is worth noting that in a recent Canadian case (*Stephens and Matchins* v. *MacMillan & MacMillan* [1954] 2 D.L.R. 135) it was held that wires placed without the necessary statutory consent across a navigable water amounted to a public nuisance.

Remedies for obstruction

An obstruction in a watercourse which amounts to a private nuisance may be abated in a reasonable manner, provided the least injurious means are employed (*Hill* v. *Cock* (1872) 36 J.P. 399), but an individual is not entitled to abate an obstruction in a navigable channel amounting to a public nuisance unless he suffers some special injury beyond that which is suffered by the rest of the public: *Colchester Corporation* v. *Brooke* (1845) 7 Q.B. 339. An obstruction which interferes with the right of access is an injury to private property and is actionable without proof of special damage: *Rose* v. *Groves* (1843) 1 Dow. & L. 61. The obstruction of the navigation of a public navigable river is a public nuisance and as such may be the subject of indictment (*R.* v. *Russell* (1827) 6 B. & C. 566) or the Attorney-General may file an information to restrain the person responsible (*A.-G.* v. *Lonsdale (Earl)* (1868) 20 L.T. 64, or ask the court for a personal decree against the defendants (*A.-G.* v. *Parmeter* (1811) 10 Price 378). In a proper case an application for *mandamus* may be made to the court: *R.* v. *Bristol Dock Co.* (1839) 1 Ry. & Can. Cas. 548.

FISHERIES

Fishing, which to some is a sport and to others a science, is a popular example of water recreation, whose origins, operations and applications are inevitably intertwined with the law, as is noted below.

Angling has ever been a popular craft through the ages, whether for the occasional enthusiast browsing over his line in some shady reach on a river convenient to town, or the fervid angler testing his skill against salmon or trout in the remoteness of Scotland or a quiet Welsh valley. Never have there been so many fishing publications, mostly profusely illustrated with fish and fly portraits, retailing the varieties of bait, tackle and the best fishing waters and recounting the niceties and methods of catching fish.

However, on turning to the legal side of fishing, it is soon discovered that there is a great lack of literature on the subject. True, one could (if you have a copy) dip into chapter 6 of Coulson and Forbes on "Waters and Land Drainage" (6th edn.) but this is a weighty tome not easily transported from the desk or library and even there the detail is not too profuse. One of the best books devoted entirely to fishery law was "The History and Law of Fisheries by S.A. and H.S. Moore – but mark the date 1903. Again, in the wake of the Salmon and Freshwater Fisheries Act, 1923, several text-books were published with annotations on the provisions of the Act, but these books sadly lack a modern edition. A new test-book on Fishery Law based on the Salmon and Freshwater Fisheries Act, 1975, is badly needed. Here it is proposed to deal briefly with certain points of the law relating to fisheries, particularly as they are affected by recent cases.

The Various Kinds of Fisheries

One of the factors which has introduced a sense of confusion into fishery law is that of classifying the different rights of fishery. Originally (one suspects), this may have been partly due to the ancient lawyers who appeared to take a positive delight in formulating difficult nomenclatures. In *Smith* v. *Kemp* (1693) 2 Salk 637, Holt, C.J. divided fisheries into:—

Separalis piscaria, i.e where the owner of the soil has the fishery;
Libera piscaria, i.e. the right of fishery without the soil;
Communis piscaria, or the right of the public to fish (in tidal waters).

But, despite the Latin names, this was an easy description compared with later efforts where one was expected to distinguish between:—

Several fisheries	Exclusive and non-exclusive fisheries
Free fisheries	Corporal and incorporated fisheries
Common of fishery	Tidal and non-tidal fisheries
Common fishery	Private and public fisheries
Fishery in gross	
Territorial fisheries	

However, as a result of several decisions, such as *Gipps* v. *Woollicot* (1697) Holt K.B. 323; *Holford* v. *Bailey* (1849) 13 Q.B. 426; *Malcomson* v. *O'Dea* (1863) 10 H.L. Cas. 593, it finally emerged that the different kinds of fisheries could be resolved down to:—

1. The public right of fishery (sometimes known as "common fishery") in the sea and tidal waters in areas not appropriated as a several fishery.
2. Several (or "free" or "exclusive") fishery, being the sole and exclusive right of one person to fish in tidal or non-tidal waters. Several fisheries are either "corporal" or "incorporeal"; a corporeal or territorial fishery exists where the right to take fish from a defined stretch of water and the soil under the water are in one ownership. Where the right to take fish is servered (either by grant or prescription) from the soil, the fishery becomes a *profit a prendre* and is known as an incorporeal fishery.
3. Common of fishery, or common piscary, may be either a right appurtenant annexed to a particular tenement such as a manor or mill, or a right in gross which is not connected with the ownership of land.

The last two classes are private rights of fishery and a useful start can be made by taking a closer look at public and private fisheries.

Public Fisheries

The public are entitled to fish on the high seas and in tidal waters (*Att.-Gen. for British Columbia* v. *Att.-Gen. for Canada* (1914) A.C. 153) and this right of fishery (as is also the right of navigation in such waters) is a public right at Common Law (*Fitzhardinge (Lord)* v. *Purcell* [1908] 2 Ch. 139), and does not depend upon any proprietary title; public fisheries in tidal waters are incorporeal. Formerly, beyond the territorial limits of the Kingdom British subjects could fish in common with the subjects of other states, save where the right has been restricted by statute and inside the territorial waters of the United Kingdom, *i.e.* within one marine league of the coast from low water mark (*vide* the Territorial Waters Jurisdiction Act, 1878), British subjects might then fish to the exclusion of other nationalities. Nowadays, through the Fishery Limits Act, 1976, British fishery limits extend up to 200 miles from the base lines from which the breadth of the territorial sea adjacent to the United Kingdom, the Channel Island's and the Isle of Man is measured, although foreign fishing boats registered in a country designated by order are authorized to fish in areas within British fishery limits designated in the order for certain descriptions of sea fish. The public right and low water marks (*Mellor* v. *Walmesley* (1905) 93 L.T. 574), except where the foreshore is vested in the owner of a several fishery.

The public right of fishery in tidal waters includes certain ancillary rights. Thus, the public may take fish and shellfish found on the shore (*Bagott* v. *Orr* (1801) 2 Bos. & P. 472), and lay lines, draw nets and use other ordinary modes of fishing; *Bevins* v. *Bird* (1865) 12 L.T. 306. But private land above high water mark cannot be used in exercising the public right of fishery, such as for drying nets or carrying fish: *Mercer* v. *Denne* [1905] 2 Ch. 538; *Ilchester (Earl)* v. *Raishleigh* (1889) 61 L.T. 477.

The public right to fish in tidal waters does not extend to non-tidal rivers, since the public have no legal right to fish in such waters, and it makes no difference if a non-tadal river is navigable: *Smith* v. *Andrews* [1891] 2 Ch. 678. Nor may a member of the public as of common right fish in canals, artificial channels or inland lakes, whatever the size: *Johnston* v. *O'Neill* [1911] A.C. 552.

Private Fisheries

A private fishery may be either a several fishery or a common of fishery, which have already been mentioned. A several fishery, being the exclusive right of one person to fish in a given place, may be contrasted with a common of fishery where the owner fishes in common with another person who enjoys the same right. Other differences are that (i) a several fishery may exist in either tidal or non-tidal waters, whereas a common of fishery is usually confined to non-tidal waters; and (ii) a several fishery is a right either with or without the property in the soil, *i.e.* it may be corporeal or incorporeal, whilst a common of fishery is incorporeal.

A private right of fishery may arise by grant, prescription, licence or lease and, in this connection, there are some recent cases on leases.

Fishing Leases

The lease of a private fishery, whether it be corporeal or incorporeal, should always be effected by deed: *Somerset (Duke)* v. *Fogwell* (1826) 5 B. & C. 875; *Fuller* v. *Brown* (1849) 13 J.P. 445. The instrument should carefully set out the respective rights and liabilities of the parties and the necessity for complete clarity in drawing up the deed is illustrated by the following cases.

Re *Vickers' Lease, Pocock* v. *Vickers* [1947] Ch. 420, C.A. concerned a lease for 21 years of the exclusive right of fishing over a length of river, and the lease contained a clause that the owner should retain for her own use a rod in the fishing. The owner died during the term of the lease and it was held that the clause conferred only a personal licence on the owner which ended with her death and did not constitute a re-grant of a *profit a prendre*.

A Canadian case, *Post* v. *Bean* [1947] 3 D.L.R. 513, emphasizes that a fishing lease must be granted for a definite term and that a lease for an uncertain period does not establish a valid tenancy. Here there was an arrangement to give the grantee fishing rights in a river without rental until certain development contemplated by the grantor took place. *Held:* this did not create an agreement capable of enforcement in the courts.

Presumptions As To Fisheries

In many branches of the law are to be found certain well-established presumptions, which are rules of construction at common law, and are *prima facie* only, liable to rebuttal on production of evidence to the contrary. Fishery law has its own share of such presumptions, which affect fisheries in both tidal and non-tidal waters.

In tidal waters there is a presumption that *prima facie* the Crown is entitled to every part of the foreshore between high and low water mark (*Fitzhardinge (Lord)* v. *Purcell* (1908) 72 J.P. 276), but opposed to this, proof of ownership of a several fishery over part of the foreshore raises the presumption against the Crown that the freehold of the soil of the fishery is vested in the owner of the fishery: *Att.-Gen.* v. *Emerson* [1891] A.C. 649.

As regards non-tidal waters, there are two presumptions regarding the ownership of the bed of a river:— (1) The right of fishery is presumptively in the several riparian owners *ad medium filum aquae* and if one person owns both banks he is entitled to the entire fishing to the extent of the length of his land (*Tracey Elliot* v. *Morley (Lord)* (1907) 51 S.J. 625); (2) where a several fishery is proved to exist the owner of the fishery is presumed to be the owner of the soil: *Hanbury* v. *Jenkins* [1901] 2 Ch. 401.

It is not always realized how difficult it is for a person to establish a claim to a right of a several fishery in tidal waters. The difficulties involved are both legal and practical.

On the legal side, first, the onus of proving his case lies on the person claiming the several fishery, because the right to fish in tidal waters is *prima facie* in the public or in the owner of the soil; *Lord Fitzwalter's Case* (1674) 3 Keb 242. Secondly, a claim to a tidal several fishery can arise only on proof either (i) that it existed before the reign of Henry II, or (ii) of long enjoyment of the fishery to the exclusion of other people of such a character as to establish that it has been dealt with as of right as a distinct and separate property, and that there is nothing to show that its origin was modern, so that a reasonable presumption is that it became such in due course of law, and therefore must have been created before legal memory: *Malcomson v. O'Dea, supra.*

The practical problems arise directly from the legal position in that much historical research and documentation is likely to be involved to indicate the history of the fishery, in producing documents of title and in proving the use and enjoyment of the fishery. If the title is in dispute, a long and costly action faces the claimant.

There is no hard and fast rule to determine how far back a claimant is obliged to go to prove a successful title. In an Irish case (*Ashworth v. Browne* (1860) 10 I.Ch.R. 421) title was proved as far back as King John, but this is exceptional. Proof of a Crown grant of a fishery by Queen Elizabeth in 1584 (*Malcomson v. O'Dea*, supra), of an inquisition taken in 1540 and identified by later documents (*Tighe v. Sinnott* [1897] 1 Ir.R. 140), and of ownership of a several fishery between 1669-1701 and 1798-1857 (*O'Neill v. Allen* (1859) 9 I.C.L. 132) are matters which the courts have held to be evidence sufficient to raise the presumption of a legal origin. But however good the paper title to a several fishery may be, it will not exclude the public right of fishery in tidal waters, without evidence of actual user and exclusive possession of the fishery by the claimant: *Neill v. Devonshire (Duke)* (1882) 8 A.C. 135.

Turning to a later case, *Stephens v. Snell* [1939] 3 All E.R. 622, the plaintiff claimed the right to a several fishery in a tidal river and sued the defendant fisherman for trespass thereon. The plaintiff based his claim on the grant of a manor including the fishery made to an abbot by either Henry I or Henry II, being monarchs who reigned before Magna Carta. Upon the dissolution of the monasteries the manor and the fishery reverted to the Crown and were subsequently regranted, after which the plaintiff's title was clear. The court decided that the plaintiff had established that the grant of the fishery had been made prior to Magna Carta and that the limits of a manorial fishery are determined by the bounds of the manor. Subsequently, in a supplementary action (*Stephens v. Snell, The Times*, 5th June, 1954) the court fixed the southern boundary of the fishery as far as the line of the mean low tide mark, although that fluctuated from time to time.

Limits of Tidal Part of Rivers

When does a river cease to be tidal and become non-tidal? This is an important question, particularly with regard to the ownership of fisheries, since the public are entitled to fish in tidal waters within the flow and reflow of the tide and the soil thereof in *prima facie* vested in the Crown (*Malcomson* v. *O'Dea*, supra), whereas in non-tidal waters the riparian owners are presumed to be the owners of the soil of the bed *ad medium filum aquae* and have the rights of fishing within such limits: *Tracey Elliot* v. *Morley (Earl)*, supra.

The line of division between the tidal and freshwater portions of rivers has been considered by the courts on a number of occasions. In *Blower* v. *Ellis* (1886) 50 J.P. 326 and *Micklethwait* v. *Vincent* (1892) 67 L.T. 225, two of the Norfolk Broads were held to be non-tidal since they were many miles from the sea where the tide did not reach, though occasionally the fresh water was backed up and rose three-quarters of an inch when there were high tides. In *Reece* v. *Miller* (1882) 47 J.P. 37, it was decided that a river was not tidal at a point where the water was not saline and unaffected by ordinary tides, although the fresh water was dammed back and caused to rise and fall by the action of the tides. See also "The History and Law of Fisheries", pp. 102-107 and *Yorkshire West Riding Rivers Board* v. *Tadcaster R.D.C.* (1907) 71 J.P. 429.

More recently and for what it is worth, the definition of the boundary between the tidal and fresh water portions of a river arose in an Irish case — *Cross* v. *Minister of Agriculture* [1941] I.R. 55. This was concerned with a Fishery Act of 1863 which gave the Minister absolute discretion so long as he acted within his jurisdiction to determine fishery boundaries in accordance with his own opinion. The Minister made his boundary between the tidal and non-tidal parts of a river on the basis of scientific tests, showing essentially fresh water vegetation growing on one side of a line and sea water vegetation on the other and the boundary marked off the fresh water portion of the river from the saline portion. *Held*: the Minister had misconstrued his statutory jurisdiction in defining the boundary as he had done; to make his statutory boundary he had to begin by ascertaining tidal limits, not saline limits. With a view to obtaining a practical result he must ascertain how far upstream the water was tidal, and take tide as the determining factor in marking out the boundary. The Minister's boundary could not be upheld. "The fresh water portion of a river means the portion which has no low water, the portion where there is no visible rise and fall, and the limits of that portion can ge ascertained only from the tide".

Fisheries and Pollution

Within the last two or three decades there have been a series of cases concerning the rights and remedies of fishery owners in respect of damage to their fisheries caused by sewage and industrial effluents discharged to rivers. These cases, which in the main merely reiterate the existing law on this aspect without establishing new principles, include *Chesham (Lord)* v. *Chesham U.D.C.* (1935) 79 S.J. 453; *Nicholls* v. *Ely Beet Sugar Factory Ltd.* 1936 Ch. 343; *Brocket (Lord)* v. *Luton Corpn.* (1948) W.N. 352; *Myddleton* v. *John Summers & Sons* [1953] C.P.L. 719; *Pride of Derby Angling Association Ltd.* v. *British Celanese Ltd.* (1953) 1 All E.R. 179. In addition, there are a couple of cases raising points of interest sufficient to deserve special mention.

It is not unknown for anglers and owners of fishing rights to take common action in defence of their legal interests through the medium of angling associations. The proper limits within which such an association may give aid in protection of his fishing interests were discussed by the court of appeal in *Martell* v. *Consett Iron Co.* [1955] 1 All E.R. 481. There a member club applied to an angling association for assistance in connexion with alleged pollution of a river by effluents from the defendants' works. The defendants applied for an injunction to stop proceedings being taken by the plaintiffs on the ground that the action was being illegally maintained by the angling association. The court decided that an association of persons individually interested as riparian owners or holders of fishing rights in the protection of the waters of rivers from pollution could, without being guilty of maintenance, lawfully support with funds at their disposal actions brought by individual members to restrain the pollution of rivers to which the interest of those members related. The offence of maintenance has since been abolished by the Criminal Law Act, 1967.

The case of *Trent River Board* v. *Sir Thomas & Arthur Wardle Ltd.*, [1957] Crim. L.R. 196: was concerned with evidence of pollution in fishery prosecutions. In the first instance, the river board laid an information in the magistrates' court against the respondents for unlawfully causing to flow into a river liquid matter to such an extent as to cause the river to be poisonous or injurious to fish, contrary to s.8(1) of the Salmon and Freshwater Fisheries Act, 1923. A water bailiff employed by the board took a sample of liquid as it fell from the point of outlet from the respondents' premises to the river, but the requirements of s.15(2) of the River Boards Act, 1948 — now replaced by s.113 of the Water Resources Act, 1963 — (which provides that the result of an analysis of a sample taken under that section shall not be admissible in evidence unless the person taking it had delivered one part of it to the occupier of the land, retained one part and submitted one part to the analyst) were not complied with.

It was agreed that as the requirements of the section had not been complied with the results of the analysis could not be given in evidence, but the board contended that they were entitled to call evidence of a qualified biologist as to the effect on fish of putting one into water containing part of the sample. The justices refused to admit this evidence and dismissed the information.

On appeal by the board by way of case stated to the Divisional Court, the Lord Chief Justice said that it might be that one simple way of proving the water was injurious would be by having an analysis made of a sample, when the provisions of s.15(2) of the Act of 1948 would apply. It was open for the prosecution to prove their case in any way they chose. His Lordship could not see that the method used by the bailiff was open to objection, as he did not make an analysis which meant dissecting the sample into its constituent parts. It was open for the prosecution to say "we saw the water coming from the defendants' premises, there a great number of fish dead in the river, we took this water and put other fish into it and they died." The justices were wrong in excluding the evidence of the biologist and the case should go back to them.

Licences to Fish

Part IV of the Salmon and Freshwater Fisheries Act, 1975, requires water authorities to issue licences to fish for salmon and trout and, unless excused, this requirement extends to freshwater fish. Any person who demands a licence and tenders the appropriate licence duty is entitled to receive a licence, unless (i) he is disqualified for holding a licence under Sch. 4, para. 9 to the Act, or (ii) a limitation has been imposed on the number of licences which can be issued (*vide* s.26). A licence may be issued to individual anglers or a general licence may be granted to any person or association of persons (such as an angling society) entitled to an exclusive right of fishing, subject to such conditions as may be agreed between the water authority and the licensee. A general licence entitles the licensee or any person authorised by him in writing to fish in any legal manner and provision is made for payment of a licence duty in respect of general licences.

In *Mills* v. *Avon & Dorset River Board* [1955] 2 All E.R. 382, the defendant board refused to grant any general licences for the year 1954 in respect of two several fisheries owned by the plaintiffs on the grounds that most of the owners of several fisheries in the board's area had commercialised their fishing and the issue of general licences extending to all persons permitted to fish by fishery owners deprived the board of revenue which they would have obtained by the issue of licences to each person who fished the waters covered by general licences. The plaintiffs had not commercialised their fisheries and applied to the court for declarations against the defendants that they were entitled to a general licence.

The court decided that a fishery owner is entitled to a general licence as of right under s.61(*g*) of the Act of 1923 (now s.25(7) of the Act of 1975) unless the board can adduce some good reason for withholding it which is referable to the applicant himself or to the conditions under which his fishery is being used; a wholesale and indiscriminate withholding of general licences was unjustified.

Fishery Boundaries

Land boundaries are usually well defined by walls, fences, hedges or ditches, or easily ascertainable by reference to marks or a plan. But water boundaries are less easy of definition (except on the bank or shoreward side), and where a property comprises part of a river or includes a portion of foreshore, the query may arise as to how the limits of the property are to be determined for the purposes of ownership. Due to the existence of two Common Law presumptions, namely:— (1) that the owner of the soil of a non-tidal river is the owner of the fishery thereover (*Lamb* v. *Newbiggin* (1844) 1 Car & Kir 549 N.P.), and (2) conversely, that the owner of a fishery is the owner of the soil of the river bed (*Holford* v. *Bailey* (1849) 13 Q.B. 426), the ascertainment of water boundaries is often synonymous with the definition of fishery boundaries — which latter is the purpose of this article.

A boundary is either the length or breadth of the limits of a fishery and, so far as the *length* or *longtitudinal boundary* (this like the expression "latitudinal boundary" hereafter quoted, is a clumsy phrase, but both are used in text books) of a fishery up and down a river is concerned, this will depend entirely upon the extent of the riparian land along the banks of the river vested in the fishery owner or claimed in respect of the fishery. Depending upon the origin of the fishery, its extent will normally be determined by the dimensions stated in the grant, conveyance, lease or other instrument giving effect to it, or by its user and enjoyment in the case of a presumed grant. In *Stephens* v. *Snell* [1939] 3 All E.R. 622, it was held that the extent in length of a manorial fishery was the bounds of the manor.

With regard to the *width* or *latitudinal extent* of a fishery, the position differs according to whether the fishery is situate on a non-tidal river, a tidal river or on the foreshore of the sea.

The right of fishing in non-tidal rivers, or in inland streams, is presumptively in the several riparian owners *ad medium filum aquae* and if the same person owns both banks he has the entire fishing to the extent of the length of his land: *Tracey Elliot* v. *Morley (Earl)* (1907) 51 S.J. 625. But this presumption in favour of a riparian owner does not arise if the fishing in his waters has been vested in other persons by grant or otherwise (*Waterford Conservators* v. *Connolly* (1889) 24 I.L.T. 7), and the presumption may be rebutted on proof of surrounding circumstances in relation to the owner's property which negative the possibility of the fishing being vested in him: *Devonshire (Duke)* v. *Patterson* (1887) 20 Q.B.D. 263. Where a private river runs through a manor, the presumption is that each landowner within the manor and on the bank of the river has the right of fishing in front of his land *ad medium filum*; if the lord of the manor claims a several fishery he must establish that claim by evidence: *Lamb* v. *Newbiggin, supra.*

In non-tidal rivers the boundary of the *medium filum aquae* has not been legally defined, but by reference to the case of *Hindson* v. *Ashby* [1896] 2 Ch. 1 C.A. (in which the American case of *Howard* v. *Ingersoll* (1851) 54 U.S. 427 was cited with approval) it appears that the *medium filum aquae*, for the purpose of boundaries of riparian land and fishing rights of respective owners on each side of the river, is a line runnding down the middle of the bed at the ordinary state of the river, i.e. the mid-line of the usual flow of the river. This expression "ordinary state of the river" can perhaps be examined more closely and exactly by comparing it with the definition ascribed to the bed of a river in another American case — *State of Alabama* v. *State of Georgia* (1859) 64 U.S. 515 — also cited in *Hindson* v. *Ashby, supra* and in *Thames Conservators* v. *Smeed* [1897] 2 Q.B. 334, namely:—

> "The bed of a river is that portion of its soil which is alternaively covered and left bare, as there may be an increase or diminution in the supply of water, and which is adequate to contain it at its average and mean stage during the entire year, without reference to the extraordinary freshets of the winter or spring, or the extreme droughts of the summer or autumn".

In tidal rivers having narrow estuaries, such as the Trent, Severn and Yorkshire Ouse, it is common (*vide* Stuart Moore on *"The History and Law of Fisheries"* (1903) at p.111) for the riparian manors (and fisheries) to extend to midstream, whereas on rivers with wider estuaries, e.g. the Thames and Humber, the manors are limited to their foreshore. In the latter case, no difficulty occurs in defining the width of the fisheries, but in rivers where the fisheries are bounded by the *filum aquae* it is possible to envisage the centre line as being the middle of the river taken at either low water or at high tide.

In *Pearce* v. *Bunting* (1896) 60 J.P. 695 — a case concerning the tidal Thames — it was held that the "shore" was distinct from the "bed", and that the latter expression was the river between low water mark on either side. But this decision was disapproved of in *Thames Conservators* v. *Smeed, supra*, where it was decided that the bed of the tidal Thames referred to the soil between ordinary high water mark on each side of the river, i.e. that it included the bed and shore.

Moore was not at all happy about the ruling in *Thames Conservators* v. *Smeed*, except so far as it defined the "bed of the Thames" for the purpose of the Thames Conservancy Acts. He contended that an estuary at full tide gave a *filum aquae* which was altogether different from a *filum aquae* at low tide. At high water the "bed" (according to the *Smeed* decision) consists of all land covered with high water at high water of ordinary tides, i.e. by the water of the sea and not the waters of the river. But at low water the land water discharges from the upper river to the sea through the low water channel which twists and winds from one side of the river to the other, and this current is "an ascertainable line by which owners of the foreshore and owners of fisheries can ascertain their boundaries by simple observation".

Moore submitted that the middle line of tidal rivers should be drawn in the middle of the stream or channel at ordinary low tide (being the water of the river, not the sea) when the tidal influence is absent and the river is discharging its waters to the sea. In support of this he quoted Hale (*De Jure Maris*, 1st Treatise, p. 354) who showed in the case of the River Severn that the middle of the stream at low water was the constant boundary of the manors on either side, and he also referred to *Miller* v. *Little* (1878) 4 L.R. Ir 302, where the river in an estuary was dealt with as a river at the low water state of the tide.

GENERAL INDEX

The user may find it helpful to refer to the entry for "Water" for guidelines to the main subjects indexed. The letter-by-letter system has been adopted.